# DOJO WISDOM

Jennifer Lawler is a writer and martial arts instructor and the author of several books including *Martial Arts for Dummies, Secrets of Tae Kwon Do,* and *Kickboxing for Women.* She has taught literature and writing at the University of Kansas, and lives in Lawrence, Kansas, with her daughter.

# Dojo Wisdom

## 100 Simple Ways to Become a Stronger, Calmer, More Courageous Person

Jennifer Lawler

PENGUIN COMPASS

PENGUIN COMPASS
Published by the Penguin Group
Penguin Group (USA) Inc., 375 Hudson Street,
New York, New York 10014, U.S.A.
Penguin Books Ltd, 80 Strand,
London WC2R 0RL, England
Penguin Books Australia Ltd, 250 Camberwell Road, Camberwell,
Victoria 3124, Australia
Penguin Books Canada Ltd, 10 Alcorn Avenue,
Toronto, Ontario, Canada M4V 3B2
Penguin Books India (P) Ltd, 11 Community Centre, Panchsheel Park,
New Delhi – 110 017, India
Penguin Books (N.Z.) Ltd, Cnr Rosedale and Airborne Roads, Albany,
Auckland, New Zealand
Penguin Books (South Africa) (Pty) Ltd, 24 Sturdee Avenue,
Rosebank, Johannesburg 2196, South Africa

Penguin Books Ltd, Registered Offices:
Harmondsworth, Middlesex, England

First published in Penguin Compass 2003

1 3 5 7 9 10 8 6 4 2

LIBRARY OF CONGRESS CATALOGING-IN-PUBLICATION DATA

Lawler, Jennifer, 1965–
Dojo wisdom / by Jennifer Lawler.
p. cm.
ISBN 0-14-219622-3
1. Martial arts.   2. Conduct of life.   I. Title.

GV1101.L385 2003
796.8—dc21        2002193118

Printed in the United States of America
Set in Guardi Roman and Gill Sans Light with Wade Sans Light
Designed by Sabrina Bowers

For my mother
(it's about time, wouldn't you say?)

# Acknowledgments

Many thanks to my friends, teachers and colleagues in the martial arts who have made the journey memorable, especially Masters Donald and Susan Booth and Grandmaster Woo Jin Jung, and all my fellow students at New Horizons Black Belt Academy of Tae Kwon Do.

Without my terrific agent, Carol Susan Roth, this book would not have existed. She championed the book and cheered me through it. Carol deserves my unending gratitude for finding me and putting up with me.

I must also thank Janet Goldstein and Ann Mah, my editors at Viking, for believing in me and in this book, and for all their assistance in making this a better book than it would have been without them.

Much appreciation to my daughter, Jessica, for giving me time to write in exchange for stickers.

Finally, special thanks are owed to Peg Strain, founder of Mona Lisa's Sword, for being there at just the right time (more than once) with generosity, kindness, and some terrific quotations; to Kerry Kilburn, a fellow martial artist and academic, for meditations on (non)violence and power; to Dena Friesen for encouragement (and childcare) from New York to Washington, DC; to Martina Sprague, a terrific martial artist and writer, who has become a supportive friend; and to Debz Buller, who always has my back.

# Contents

# Introduction

I am a woman warrior. The first fact is pertinent to the second. For centuries, only men have trained to become warriors, and discounted attempts by women to do the same. A warrior rode off onto a field of battle and returned victorious (or maybe didn't return at all.) Women and children waited at home.

But our understanding of what it means to be a warrior has changed. Anyone can be a warrior, regardless of gender, or age, or background. I have seen twelve-year-old warriors and seventy-year-old warriors. I have seen deaf warriors and warriors with multiple sclerosis. My five-year-old daughter, who has multiple disabilities, is a warrior. She has taught me much about what it means to be a warrior amidst chaos and pain.

There is no set standard for what makes a warrior. You don't have to be able to throw people over your shoulder or endure a fifty-mile forced march. That's not what being a warrior means. Being a warrior means living with courage and integrity, and facing difficulties with dignity, and finding joy even in sorrow.

When I began training in martial arts more than ten years ago, I was oddly unformed for a twenty-seven-year-old. I was single and in graduate school. That was about all you could say for certain about me. I was unassertive, a walking doormat. I quit everything I ever tried. I had dreams but not the courage to pursue them.

Now I am the divorced mother of a charming daughter. I teach martial arts to children with special needs as well as to other children and adults. I have written and published seventeen books, with more forthcoming. I earned a Ph.D. in medieval English literature and a black belt in Tae Kwon Do. People who watch me train think I am one of the most intensely focused individuals they have ever met.

With the exception of my daughter, none of that matters as much to me as this: One day, a martial artist I truly admire and respect turned to me and said, "You have true warrior spirit."

I have always wanted to be a warrior.

Being a warrior isn't about learning how to kick people five different ways. Being a warrior is about how you live your life. Before I became a warrior, my life was frustrating, unrewarding and unfulfilling. I didn't know what I wanted or how I might get there. Now my life is full and happy, with many challenges and rewards. I seldom have moments of feeling down, when once I felt engulfed by despair. Becoming a warrior did not change my life. It saved my life.

To become a warrior means learning certain lessons. It means learning how to be civil and courteous to others, learning to respect and appreciate your gifts, learning to define what you want, not labor under the expectations of others. What these lessons are and how you can learn them is what *Dojo Wisdom* is about. I hope you too can save your life by becoming a warrior.

And remember, the most important lesson ever is this: We can *all* be warriors.

Dojo Wisdom

# 1

"If you know the art of breathing, you have the strength, wisdom and courage of ten tigers."

—OLD CHINESE ADAGE

Learning to harness your breathing gives you control over your Chi or life force, what might be called your "inner energy." People with strong Chi have vibrant personalities and an excess of energy, a lot like a Labrador puppy or a full-grown Alaskan malamute.

Breathing correctly, on a simple biological basis, helps oxygenate your blood, which in turn gives you more energy. Therefore, breathing correctly when you exert yourself gives you endurance—and the strength of ten tigers.

On a more esoteric level, breathing helps you center yourself and tap into your Chi, which is located in your abdomen. By breathing correctly when you exert yourself, you can use your Chi to give yourself more focus and energy.

Breathing techniques can also be used to help you calm down and de-stress as well as to help you meditate. The ability to reduce and control your stress level on demand helps you deal with challenges of all kinds—for instance, training the aforementioned Lab to sit when you say so. Breathing to aid meditation helps you gain insight into yourself and the world around you—thus, you will develop the wisdom and courage of ten tigers.

Martial artists (and other athletes) use many different kinds of breathing techniques, depending on their particular needs, but to begin, your basic goal should be to simply become conscious of your breathing. Most of the time, we take very shallow breaths. This does not give us the energy we need for physical action or to cope with stressful situations. Instead, concentrate on breathing deeply so your chest and abdomen visibly expand. Then focus on expelling most (not all) of the air from your lungs to make way for a fresh intake of breath.

Notice your breathing when you're stressed. It's probably quick and shallow. Also, notice your breathing when you're exerting yourself—walking, running, stair climbing. It's probably irregular. When this happens, concentrate on finding a rhythm for your breathing. This helps you relax and gives you more endurance. When you exert yourself, you can push a little harder if you focus on your breathing. This focus on breath helps you tap into your Chi; your breath becomes the physical embodiment of your Chi.

### Exercise

Next time you feel tense, practice simple focused breathing. Inhale deeply through your nose, filling your lungs to capacity. Then breathe slowly out through your mouth. Do this technique ten times, breathing in and out more slowly with each successive breath. This focused breathing technique can also be used to help you recover more quickly after physical exertion. You can return your heart rate to normal much faster if you spend a few moments doing focused breathing after a workout. This gives you the energy to get on with your day even after you've put forth tremendous physical effort.

Once you're comfortable with this technique, try "push hands" breathing technique, used in Chinese martial arts. Lift your arms so that they're parallel to the floor, keeping your shoulders back. This allows your lungs and chest plenty of room to expand and fill. Take a deep breath. Then bend your elbows and slowly push your palms together, exhaling as you push. Feel the air entering your body and energizing your blood; feel your body expel the used air along with all of your tension and stress. Again, progressively slow your breathing with each repetition of the technique. This breathing exercise will not only relieve stress, but it will also help you empty your mind and prepare for meditation or visualization.

## 2

# A punch is just a punch

Bruce Lee once said (to paraphrase) that before he began training in martial arts, a punch appeared to be just a punch—that is, a tool for fending off an attacker. But when he began to study martial arts, the punch became much more—it became symbolic of power, of control, of possibility, of achievement. Yet, when he finally understood martial arts, he realized that a punch was just a punch. A tool for fending off an attacker.

This is true of many objects and concepts, not just kicks and punches. When we look at the surface of a thing, we believe we understand its basic nature. But when we study the thing more closely, we realize that it includes infinite mysteries. Yet, once we understand the essence of a thing, we understand its basic nature, which may be that it is exactly what it appears to be.

To apply this principle to life: Perhaps you meet a person who appears to be the strong, silent type. You suspect that underneath the gruff, unpolished exterior there is a deep intellect and many unexpressed emotions. But you should not be surprised if it turns out that the person is only interested in body building and doesn't have much to say. A punch is just a punch.

We often project our own needs and desires onto the objects and people around us. It is important to know the difference between what a thing really is and what we want it to be: Are we truly seeing or are we seeing only what we want to see? Is a punch an expression of personal empowerment or is it just a means for giving an attacker a big old bruise? It's possible that an object or concept can be both at the same time, but we need to set aside our interpretations and see what a thing truly is before we make a judgment.

### Exercise

Consider something that you like. Perhaps you like daffodils. Make a list of all the reasons you like that thing. Maybe daffodils remind you of spring, and mean that winter is over; maybe your first boyfriend bought a bunch for you when you were newly in love; maybe they were the first flower you learned to grow. Then consider what of these attributes are naturally intrinsic in the nature of the daffodil. You'll see that we often heap objects (and people) with meanings far beyond their actual nature. It can be a tough load for a daffodil to carry. Look at the daffodil, stripped of its load of meanings, and think about its nature, its essence. It's a beautiful growing flower. Maybe that's all it has to be.

### 3

# Revel in your awkwardness as much as in your mastery

Zen Buddhists teach that keeping a beginner's mind is essential to enlightenment. A beginner's mind is open and accepting.

But everyone wants to be a master. There's a reward to being a master—prestige or status or respect or maybe a good job. Usually, we want to be masters instantly because we're motivated by the associated prestige or status. As a rule, we don't think there's much that's good about the beginner's mind. When you're trying to figure out why you keep getting the same error message every time you turn on your computer, it's a little hard to feel pleased about your beginner's mind. You don't feel open and accepting. You feel like throwing your computer through the nearest window.

But as you learn something new—how to use a new program, how to perform a plié in ballet—you should enjoy your awkwardness. That's right, you should enjoy what an idiot you are. Think about how long you've been inhabiting this body and laugh at how hard it is to make said body perform a plié. When you enjoy this awkwardness, you're not censoring and criticizing yourself. You're allowing yourself to learn. If you focus only on the negative—that you can't do something very well, that the computer is still smarter than you, that you aren't a master yet—then you will feel only frustration and resentment and may abandon the project or throw the computer through the nearest window even though you're still making payments on it.

As you learn how to do a skill, you'll feel a sense of satisfaction and delight. You didn't know you could do it! Once you've mastered a skill, however, those feelings of exhilaration are replaced by a calm, confident acceptance. While that calm, confident acceptance is certainly enjoyable and it should be your goal, those feelings of exhilaration will never be recaptured. They were part of the learning process. Yet, if you never experienced that rush of satisfaction, because you were mired in frustration at your beginner mistakes, you missed one of the best parts of learning, that "I can do it!" exultation.

By embracing the awkwardness instead of fearing it or being embarrassed by it, you'll be more likely to try new things and attempt new skills instead of being scared off by the learning process. You'll enjoy learning and you'll create less stress for yourself. You'll feel the joy of growing, if you can keep your beginner's mind.

Exercise

When faced with a task you haven't mastered, consciously think about what is making you feel frustrated. Laugh at the absurdity of the situation. If you fall down doing the jump spinning wheel kick, at least you're trying the jump spinning wheel kick (trust me, plenty of people aren't). And isn't it funny that you're frustrated over *that*?

Next time you turn on the computer program that you can't figure out how to use, don't tense up and feel frustrated. Accept that you still have things to learn. Don't feel defensive when you have to call and ask your son yet again how to open the file you're trying to work on. Know that someday you won't have to ask for help again. Keep that beginner's mind—open, uncritical, accepting—for as long as you can.

4

# Use your attacker's momentum against him or her

A well-known Aikido principle states that you never meet force with more force. Instead, you simply redirect your attacker's force, deflecting it from yourself. If you're good enough, you can actually use your attacker's momentum against him or her. So even though the loud-mouthed drunk person at the other end of the bar actually meant to punch you in the nose for being a Raiders fan, *he's* the one who ends up on the floor wondering what happened.

An important aspect of this principle is to do the least amount of harm to an attacker while still stopping the attack. This is a prudent approach, considering how often people get sued by the very criminals they were attempting to defend themselves against.

An attacker doesn't have to be a loud-mouthed drunk

person at the end of the bar who doesn't like Raiders fans. And an attack doesn't have to consist of a punch to the nose.

Instead of responding to an attack (your mother criticizes your ten-year-old's table manners) with an attack of equal force (if your mother could cook, your kid wouldn't feel compelled to feed the meal to the dog under the table), you yield. This doesn't mean you need to imitate a doormat. ("You're right, I'm a terrible mother and he eats like a pig.") It can mean that you simply redirect the conversation. ("This isn't the time or place to discuss it.") It can mean you laugh off the criticism. ("Aren't kids impossible? I was a handful, too, wasn't I?") You can quietly respond with a request to stop the attack. ("I would appreciate not hearing a lot of criticism while we're having a family get-together.") Or you could ask for advice—everybody loves to give advice. ("How did you teach me my lovely table manners? I don't really remember and I'm afraid our little Jason resists our best attempts.") For this approach to work, it's best not to be too sarcastic when you say it.

By not responding to an attack with an equal attack, you prevent an unpleasant encounter from turning into fodder for the lawyers. This principle can be applied to practically any conflict you have in your daily life.

### E x e r c i s e

The next time someone seems intent on starting an argument, refuse to argue. This is, of course, hard. (If it were easy, there would be no arguments.) When a person criticizes you for an idea or a belief, don't automatically counterattack. Insist that the other person treat you with respect. ("Stop shouting so we can talk about it.") Refuse to be baited. Leave the room if you must. But don't get into the argument. Ask, "What am I doing that makes you angry?" and "What can I do to fix the problem?" It may be that there's nothing you can do, or you're unwilling to do what is asked, but that doesn't need to be the focus. Redirect the attacker's energy into finding a constructive solution.

If this is not possible, tell the attacker that you'll discuss it when he or she is sane and rational, but you won't talk about it now. Occasionally, your calm behavior will incense the attacker more, in which case you simply continue to refuse to argue, leaving the attacker alone. Often, though, your calm behavior will make the other person aware that he or she has lost control, is acting like a child, and needs to grow up. You'll often get an apology out of it (although you don't want to count on this).

## 5
## Know the vital points, strike to the vital points

The human body has vulnerable points, weak spots that, when attacked, can seriously injure (possibly kill) a person. For example, a person's throat is a vulnerable spot. A sharp blow to the throat can cause extensive injury. The nose is easily broken; fragments of cartilage can be driven into the brain, causing serious injury (although this is rare). A man's genitals are a vulnerable spot. A kick to a man's privates won't kill him but it can make him whimper.

These vulnerable areas, called vital points, are your

targets when you're trying to disable an attacker. Kicking someone in the hip or the abdomen isn't going to be as effective as gouging her eyes.

When you're under attack, you must stop the attack. If you can do so without damaging yourself or your attacker, this is obviously ideal. But there are many times when you have one shot at stopping a violent attack and that's when you kick the attacker where it counts.

If you try to fight an attacker without knowing what his vital points are, you'll spend a lot of time kicking hard and doing very little damage. If you have only one shot, and you don't have a clue as to what your attacker's vital points might be, you're not likely to land a disabling blow.

Know the vital points. Focus on them. Don't waste your energy on other targets. If you want to be promoted to manager, and you know that only people with college degrees are ever promoted to manager, then you need to earn a college degree. Babysitting your boss's toddler twins is not the vital point. (Brown-nosing can be an effective strategy but it won't always get you where you want to go.) In the same way, complaining about this policy is pointless. Spend your energy getting the degree.

If your attacker has a weakness, exploit it. When you're in the ring, you're not allowed to strike to certain vital points because they are so dangerous. For example, there's no hitting below the belt. And you can't gouge out your opponent's eyes. But you can exploit your opponent's weaknesses. If a boxer opens up a cut on her opponent's cheek, she doesn't stop hitting the cheek. In fact, she starts hitting it harder. If your opponent isn't able to counter your roundhouse kick effectively, you keep throwing the roundhouse kick.

If you're in the running for a promotion, and your main competition has more experience and a more impressive college education than you do, don't focus on these achievements, seeing only where you come up short. Instead, consider her weaknesses and try to make those your strengths. For instance, she may make a habit of taking long lunch breaks. Keep yours shorter. She may be rude to the secretarial help. You should be respectful and considerate. If you're asked why you should be chosen for the promotion, you don't say, "Because Suzy takes long lunches and I don't." Instead, you say, "Because I work hard and give my best effort; I try not to be distracted from getting my job done. I get so involved sometimes I even forget to have lunch!"

Don't say, "Even though I don't have much experience . . ." You're not striking to your vital points, you're striking to someone else's. Don't emphasize where you're vulnerable; know where your opponent is vulnerable.

### E x e r c i s e

Consider a goal or challenge in your life that has been problematic. Perhaps you keep getting passed over for promotion. Learn what the vital points are. Talk it over with your supervisor or a trusted colleague. ("What can I do to make myself more attractive for the next promotion opportunity?") Boil the information you receive down to the essentials.

It might be that you need more project management experience. It might be that the people you supervise complain that you're abrasive and heavy-handed. It might be that you're only marginally competent in your current position. It doesn't matter. Don't let the criticism hurt your feelings. (I've been only marginally competent at more than one job, and I still managed to make a success of my career.) Work to better these areas. Focus on them. If no one criticizes your supervisory skills, then don't spend a lot of sleepless nights worrying about them. But if everyone agrees that you need to learn to add before you become Chief Engineer, learn to add. Then make certain everyone knows what you've done to improve your skills.

## 6
## You are worth defending

When I first began teaching martial arts, I showed a woman who had just started taking lessons the basic techniques, including what's called a "two-finger strike," a jab with the index and middle fingers to the attacker's eyes.

The student recoiled and said, "Oh, I don't think I could actually hurt anyone!"

"But," I tried to explain reasonably, "you use this technique if someone is trying to hurt *you*."

She looked doubtful. "I wouldn't mind learning how to get away from an attacker. But I could never hurt someone else."

I was surprised, but later I found that many women (and some men) feel this way. While an instinct to avoid causing pain is admirable, and avoiding the necessity of doing so is ideal, there are times when an attacker just isn't going to listen to reason, and you have to be prepared to punch him in the nose (or gouge him in the eyes.) Refusing to cause physical harm to others may be the goal of a pacifist, but these people who didn't want to hurt anyone weren't pacifists. If you asked them, "What if someone were hurting your child or your elderly parent?" they would invariably respond that yes, in that case, they would be able to hurt an attacker if there were no other way to stop the attack. In fact, they could get pretty lurid in their descriptions of what they'd do to someone who hurt their child.

Even if you would choose, for moral or ethical reasons, not to inflict injury on another person, being *incapable* of doing so does not make you morally or ethically superior. Being capable of violence but choosing not to use violence is actually the position a pacifist takes. Choosing not to and not knowing how are two different things.

In most cases, the people I teach don't have an ethical reason not to defend themselves. They just feel uncomfortable with the concept. They think they're not worth it. They think someone can hurt them, but they have no right to hurt that person in self-defense.

This attitude is, sadly, prevalent among women who are willing to do anything to keep their kids or their dog free from harm, but just don't feel entitled to do the same for themselves . . . as if saving themselves from harm was somehow selfish. Many self-defense instructors give in to this cultural assumption and say, "Pretend you're fighting for your child." Some of the more enlightened say, "If you're hurt, you won't be there for your kid, your dog Rover, your elderly parents." But this still implies that you're not important in and of yourself. The truth is, just by reason of existing, you have a right to exist free from harm.

In other words, you should learn to defend yourself because you're worth defending.

You are worth defending.

It won't always be a mugger who wants to drag you down an alley that you have to defend yourself against. In fact, you don't often have to do that. If you're a woman, you're far more likely to have to defend yourself against someone you know, a boyfriend who doesn't listen when you say "no," the neighbor who comes over to fix your leaky sink and reads more into the situation than exists.

The threat isn't always physical, either. It might be a threat to your dignity or self-esteem, such as when your boss tells an off-color joke at work, or your father belittles your abilities. Letting people get away with this behavior simply reinforces the message that you're not worth defending—both to them and to you. If you stand up to this, you teach yourself that you're worth defending, and it becomes easier to do with each successive event. And it also teaches people that you won't put up with their disrespectful behavior, and they'll stop doing it. Usually.

### Exercise

The next time your boss or co-worker tells an off-color joke, or someone insults you, don't tell yourself that only a jerk would draw attention to the behavior. (The jerk is the person engaged in the behavior.) Simply but firmly say, "I don't find that kind of humor amusing." Or, "Don't insult me. I would appreciate an apology."

You may be accused of having no sense of humor . . . you may even be accused (as I have been) of *creating* conflict. But off-color jokes aren't funny at work, and an insult directed at you is *already* a belligerent act. You're just identifying it and bringing it out into the open.

By exercising your right to defend yourself, you will teach people to treat you with respect and consideration. You are worth defending.

## 7

# Locate and summon your Chi

Your Chi is your inner energy or life force. Traditionalists believe it is located in your abdomen and can be summoned at will; it can even be expelled from your body to affect objects outside your body (for example, like the dreaded *dim mak* death touch by which all you have to do is touch someone with your Chi to make him keel over).

Whether you think of Chi as an entity shared and used by all living creatures, or as simply a shorthand method for saying "focus and execution," you should know how to find and use your Chi. If it remains hidden inside you, it's not doing you much good.

You should be able to focus at a moment's notice. This ability only comes through practice in using your Chi. In martial arts, a practitioner might take a deep breath, focus her will or her Chi, and then strike the target. The target might be a board she's breaking or an opponent in the ring. By physically expressing her Chi, she's learning to harness it and use it. Once she has experienced this, she will be able to summon and use her Chi even when she doesn't need to strike physically. She can use her Chi for emotional and mental challenges.

Summoning your Chi helps you relax during stressful periods. It helps give you the energy you need to get through a trying day without yelling at the kids too much. But one of the most important things Chi does is give you the ability to add power, intensity and focus to achieving your goals.

Consider the series of steps you take when you want to focus on something. Maybe you find a place to be alone, shut the door, turn off the radio, and concentrate only on the task at hand. Now, think about how to attain that level of concentration without having to be alone with the door shut and the radio off. Find your Chi by being able to tune out all distractions, except the task at hand. (Fighters repeatedly say that when they get in the ring, they can no longer hear the crowd, or even their trainer. All they can see and hear is their opponent. They have learned to focus at a moment's notice, despite plenty of distractions.)

Imagine you're an emergency room physician. An ambulance pulls up, discharging an injured patient on a stretcher. At the same time, the patient's parents show up, demanding to know the status of the patient, the triage nurse is trying to assess the severity and nature of the patient's injuries, and the two paramedics are telling you what happened.

If you're that ER physician, you can't say to the paramedics, "Listen, let's grab a cup of coffee and find a quiet spot in the cafeteria to talk this case over." You have to focus on the patient, listen to the paramedics, then give the nurse your orders. You have to ask the parents to be patient while you do your job. That requires focus—finding your Chi and using it. If you feel stressed out and panicky, you won't handle the situation well, and you won't be able to respond to events and priorities in their proper order.

In the short term, you might feel frustrated trying to concentrate when other distractions vie for your attention, but in the long run, you'll have more command of your life and you'll be more disciplined. Short-term frustration in exchange for long-term competence is a fair barter.

### Exercise

Use breathing to help you find your Chi. Take a deep breath. Feel the air fill your lungs. Expand your chest and abdomen. Feel the center of your abdomen (I mean that literally; go ahead and touch your abdomen, pushing gently just above the navel. There's your Chi.) Then expel the breath slowly through your mouth. Feel the strength and energy you expel. That's summoning your Chi.

Now, make the expulsion of breath coincide with a physical effort—punching a heavy bag, lifting a heavy object. Intensely experience that feeling. Now you're using your Chi.

When faced with a non-physical task, recapture that feeling of strength and focus by breathing deeply and consciously. (This will also reduce your heart rate and make you feel less stressed.)

## 8

# The sound of your shout
## gives you power

One physical expression of Chi is the shout, called a *kiai* (key-i) or *kihop,* depending on whether you're practicing a Japanese or a Korean martial art. Martial artists use the shout when they break boards or while sparring. The shout focuses their Chi, gives them energy and determination and can disorient the hell out of an attacker.

I am known as "the *kihop* lady." People know I'm practicing martial arts just by listening. "Jennifer must be in there," they'll say as they walk by the *dojo* (training hall). "I can hear her."

I love having a loud, intense shout, and not just because it intimidates the lower belts. I love having a loud, intense shout because it makes me powerful.

When I shout *"HIYA!!!"* I know I can do anything. My blood rushes, my mind focuses, and that opponent is history, baby. I exult in my shout.

It wasn't always this way. When I began training, I was terribly embarrassed at the thought of shouting. Nice girls don't draw attention to themselves in public. My instructor encouraged me, though. "Now, shout when you punch," he would say. I would say, "Hi? ya?" and strike a feeble blow.

Many beginners are exactly like this. Over time, they learn to have fun with their shout. They learn, like I did, that it's okay if the shout draws attention. In fact, the shout should.

When I shout, and people stare at me, I always smile at them (this would be my evil smile) and they know what I'm thinking. I'm thinking, "and I can kick your ass, too." So the shout is a real confidence builder. It's also a self-defense tool.

Department of Justice statistics show that as many as 50 percent or more of all attempted assaults are stopped—*stopped*—when the intended victim uses his or her voice. I don't know a single self-defense technique that has a success rate as high as that. Shouting "No!" is most effective. But "Help!" or "Fire!" or "Get away from me, you twerp!" will also discourage an assailant.

Learning to shout also makes you more comfortable raising your voice in other circumstances, such as when no one is listening to you, or when they interrupt you, or when they try to drown you out. A loud, intense, "NO!" will get you heard every time.

### Exercise

Embarrassment at shouting knows no age or gender. I've had men and women, adults and children, tell me they're just not comfortable shouting. Since I don't like to lose students, I don't say things like, "Tough cookies, shout anyway." I just keep encouraging them and keep modeling it. Pretty soon they decide if I'm willing to sound like a fool, they are, too.

Many people scream rather than shout. But a scream or a shriek or a screech is a sign of fear, not a sign of confidence and dominance. It does not carry conviction the way a shout does.

The scream comes from using your lungs to yell. The shout—the *kihop*—comes from using your Chi.

To find your *kihop*, inhale deeply. As you exhale, make a long sound, like "ahhhh" or "mmmm." Using your fingers, press your abdomen a few inches above your navel. You should feel your breath forcefully expelled and your "ahh" or "mmm" suddenly becomes louder and stronger. Visualize this spot. This is where your shout comes from. Summon your shout from deep within you and you will roar like a lion.

## 9
## Strike through the target

When you're a martial artist trying to break a board (or defeat an attacker, or win a competition), you learn to use focus and correct technique to achieve your goal. But no matter how much focus you have and no matter how good your technique, if you think hitting the board (striking the target) will accomplish your goal (breaking the board), you'll be disappointed. Striking the target just means sore knuckles.

Instead, you have to strike *through* the target. You have to aim beyond the board in order to break it. Otherwise, your strike stops at the board, the board absorbs the power of the strike (and sits there, unbroken, while people grin at you).

To strike through the target, you see the board, but you don't aim for the board; you aim slightly beyond the board. To get to that place on the other side of the board requires focus, power and technique. It requires your total commitment for the few seconds it takes to perform the break. If you strike through the target, you will break the board, achieving your goal.

- If you focus on the board, you can be afraid of the board. But if you think of the board as just a nuisance, just an obstacle on the way to your real goal, then it's not so intimidating.
- Too often, we see a target, set a goal, but forget to follow through. It is in the follow-through that you succeed. You might decide you have a goal of losing twenty pounds by summer, but unless you follow through, you will still be twenty pounds overweight when June comes along.
- We often set goals without looking to see what is beyond them. We see the target—selling 500 widgets, graduating from college, publishing a first novel—without thinking about what happens next. If all your effort goes to selling 500 widgets, and you're so exhausted by the effort that you can't produce the 500 widgets, you're in trouble. If all your life you've dreamed of publishing a novel, and then your novel gets published, now what? Is that it? By looking beyond the target, we can often see what we're really aiming at. (If I get my novel published, I can quit my job selling widgets and earn the respect of my peers.)
- Sometimes we set our sights too low. If your goal is to sell 500 widgets this year, and you

meet your goal, fine. But maybe your co-worker set her sights on selling 5,000 widgets this year. Even if she doesn't achieve her goal, and only gets halfway there, she has still sold a lot more widgets than you have.

Exercise

Look at the boards you want to break (the goals you want to achieve.) Write them down, starting with the most important. Ask yourself if you have correctly identified your goals. (Remember, *striking* the board is not the goal; *breaking* the board is the goal.) For each goal, ask yourself "Why?" Why is it important to get accepted at Yale, or to land a job at the law firm downtown? What unstated goals are propping up your stated goals?

You may see that a goal you're aiming for won't result in what you really want. Or you might see that your unstated goal can be achieved another way, which means it won't be such a disaster if you don't get admitted to Yale.

Ask yourself what happens when you achieve your goals. What's next? This is a scary prospect, but you can't ignore it. So what happens when the board breaks? Do you just keep breaking boards? Do you up the ante, by breaking concrete blocks instead of boards? Or do you appreciate your achievement and decide it might be interesting to try fire walking instead? There's no right answer, of course; you just have to ask the question.

## 10

# You cannot spar from five feet away

When martial artists begin training, they're introduced to the basic techniques of their style: kicks, punches, blocks (or sweeps, throws, and joint locks). They practice these techniques by kicking and punching the air (like a boxer shadowboxing) or perhaps by striking a heavy bag or a padded target. But they can't do this forever. Sooner or later, they have to try out their techniques against a live partner—a sparring partner.

Once the instructor feels the beginner has gained a basic understanding of a few techniques, the beginner is paired with a partner and shown how to engage in mock combat—that is, to use a variety of techniques (kicks and punches, sweeps and throws) to score a point (strike to an unblocked target area; pin the partner to the mat).

This is much scarier than it sounds. First, there's the chance that you could get hit (and it might hurt to get hit!). Then there's the chance you might hit your partner (and it might hurt your partner to get hit!).

Beginners do not feel they have very good control over their bodies. They're not convinced that they could block their partner's kicks and punches, and they're not convinced they could kick and punch the partner without hurting him or her. So to solve this problem, beginners invariably spar from five feet away.

If you and your partner cannot touch each other, no one will get hurt.

Of course, no sparring will actually take place, either.

You have to get in range to spar. To score a point, you have to risk hitting the other person. You have to risk getting hit.

The analogy applies to many of our daily experiences. If we stay five feet away, we won't get hurt, we won't get involved, we won't run any risks. Of course, we won't actually experience anything, either. . . .

## E x e r c i s e

To be truly joyful and courageous in your life requires engagement. You have to get out there and do it. Think of something you'd like to try but haven't because you think you'll look stupid or you might make a fool of yourself (all beginning martial artists look pretty silly when they start sparring . . . they're all flinches and huge exaggerated movements). Maybe you'd like to learn to line dance, or you've always wanted to take ballet lessons, or just once you'd like to sing Karaoke with your friends. Give yourself permission to get in there and do something even if it involves some risk to your ego or your pretensions. Once you've done the little thing and survived, it'll be easier to take the bigger risks . . . and earn the greater rewards.

## 11

# Accept criticism and correction

The nice thing about adulthood is that nobody can tell you what to do anymore. Sort of. Of course, your boss tells you what to do, and your mom has the occasional suggestion, and you do obey the laws of the land, but beyond that, you are your own person.

But part of becoming a better person—or simply reaching your goals, if you're not interested in becoming a better person—is learning to accept criticism and correction.

This doesn't mean you should sit by meekly while your boss tells you everything that's wrong with you. It means you can't learn if you're not willing to find out what you're doing wrong.

A martial artist does not attend the first training session and perform a front kick perfectly. No. In fact, she performs only a vague approximation of a front kick. If no one ever criticized her front kick—corrected her technique—she'd have a poor front kick forever, and a lot of good that would do her in the sparring ring.

She won't get the front kick right on the second try or the second class or even the second month. But she'll keep getting closer. Even when she's a black belt, she'll still be mastering the front kick, but it'll be a lot more effective than the front kick she had on the first day of training.

The minute she decides her front kick is perfect is the

minute she stops learning how to make it better. So it's important to keep your mind open and your heart willing when you're learning something new—or even when you're practicing something old.

When I teach beginners, I can usually tell those who have had martial arts training before. They fall into two types: those who are comfortable and confident about their bodies but otherwise just want you to show them what you know about martial arts, and those who have decided they know all about martial arts and what you're teaching them is not what they know, so you must be wrong. Guess which type of student lasts the longest and learns the most?

Not all correction and criticism is worthwhile or justified. Unwarranted criticism can be dealt with firmly. ("I disagree that having a tummy tuck will save our marriage. If you feel our marriage needs work, let's talk to a counselor.")

Your teachers don't have to be people you hire to show you how to perform that radical jump reverse axe kick. They can be your kids, your dog, the cranky old man who lives down the street. If you're open to what they have to teach you, you can become better. More confident, more accomplished, happier.

If you don't want to hear it, you're losing out on many opportunities to grow.

Exercise

The next time someone criticizes you—for example, at your next employee evaluation—don't immediately flare up and become defensive or point out that the person criticizing you has shortcomings, too. Listen respectfully without saying anything. Don't even think about what you're going to say. Just listen. Consider, as objectively as you can, what they've said. If any actual facts are incorrect, point them out—respectfully. ("You say I have been absent five times this month. According to my records, I have only been gone three times. However, I realize that is still excessive and will work to do better.")

You can also correct any errors in interpretation, again keeping calm. ("You say that my missing this much work means I'm not committed to my job. I am very committed to my job, but in fact my son has been quite ill. I see now that I need to have a backup plan so that I don't have to miss work when he's sick. I will also do better to communicate these problems to you so that you don't misunderstand what is happening.")

In neither case do you tell your boss what a big fat idiot she is.

You accept the criticism. If you've missed too much work, you've missed too much work. State how you plan to improve your performance so that you're certain you understood the criticism and that you recognize the solution to the problem.

Listen, don't respond defensively, and try to see how you can build on criticism to improve your performance.

## 12
# Hone your tools through continual sharpening

If you learn how to do a side kick, but then stop practicing it, when the mugger comes you may still be able to do a side kick (which is better than nothing), but it won't be your best, most effective side kick. Your tools need continual sharpening to remain effective.

You know what I mean. You took high school French ten years ago but haven't spoken it since. *Parlez-vous Français?*

Probably *non*.

Often, once we've mastered a skill (or at least know how to do it), we grow lazy about it. We memorized the times table once upon a time but have been using a pocket calculator ever since. We used to beat all comers at the annual spelling bee, but now are fortunate to have spell-check on our computer programs.

Any skill requires practice to remain useful. So dust off those Rollerblades, or break out the accounting textbooks, and brush up on the fundamentals.

Don't assume that just because you once learned something, you'll never forget it. Make time to keep those skills sharp.

And don't forget that you have more than one set of tools. Often, we neglect some aspects of our lives to focus on others. We might keep our minds in shape but lead sedentary lives. We might stay in shape physically and mentally but forget that emotionally and spiritually we need work sometimes. A warrior is a lifelong learner and a lifelong practitioner. Hone your tools through continual sharpening.

Exercise

Consider an area of your life where you feel a little foggy in your knowledge. Haven't solved for $x$ in twenty years? Deliberately spend some time practicing this. You'll feel exhilarated. You'll practically hear those synapses firing again. If you're a physician, crack open a basic biology text just to refresh your memory. If you're a tennis player, practice your serve for three hours or have your partner lob balls to your backhand all morning. In short, get back to the basics and remember how it's really done.

## 13
# Do not push when you mean to strike

When new martial artists hit the heavy bag or try to break a board, they often do their technique correctly in most respects—except they push instead of strike.

They push the heavy bag away. They push the board away. In neither case are they generating very much power.

Power does not come just from mass. It also comes from speed. Pushing something may require you to use mass, but it doesn't require speed. By hitting a target quickly—striking it—you create more power than you can achieve from mere mass alone.

So to be successful, you need to be strong *and* fast. (Of course, mass and strength are not exactly the same thing, but people with more mass tend to have more strength than people with less mass; people with less mass can build more strength through resistance training.) If you hit the board fast and you hit it hard, the board will break. If you hit it fast but with no power—if you slap it—it won't break. Strikes require both strength and speed.

Consider how this works in business. A successful multinational manufacturing company has mass. It's strong. But it ain't quick. When an opportunity arises, the management takes it under advisement. The company pushes and can be successful the way a steamroller is successful. Sheer mass can overwhelm the competition, especially if the competition is unduly impressed by mass.

Take, on the other hand, a typical tech company. It's fast. It's so quick you can hardly keep up. New opportunities? On 'em faster than you can say "innovation." But such a tech company is like a slap. It doesn't have the experience, the team, the capitalization—in short, the mass—to be successful long term. A company that relies on quick can be successful, especially in the short term, because all that slapping can be annoying and distracting to the competition, who never knows what the company is going to do next. This gives the illusion that the tech company is a leader, is in charge.

But more and more business leaders are finding that, long term, the most successful companies are those that strike—that have power and speed—that can take advantage of an opportunity but not every opportunity, and that also have the resources and infrastructure to support ongoing programs or to go into battle with the competition.

## Exercise

The next time you need to take action, do not push when you mean to strike. Consider what needs to be done, assess your resources, make a decision and act. Don't spend endless time debating the correct course of action; at the same time, don't move quickly and ineffectively, which will waste resources.

Suppose your relationship with your husband seems to be in trouble. Immediately filing for divorce might be the quick answer, but it might not be the best answer. Complaining endlessly to your sister might not be the best answer either. Instead, consider the alternatives, such as counseling (either jointly or on your own) or a trial separation. Your options will depend partly on your spouse. If you bring up counseling and he won't go, you may be able to make some headway by going to counseling yourself, but it will be hard to save your marriage unless both parties are equally committed.

Once you decide on a course of action, do it immediately. If you decide on joint counseling, then start that week. Don't wait to see if things will get better on their own. Strike before it's too late.

## 14

# Learn to bow and you will stand tall

Traditional martial arts teach practitioners to bow to each other, to senior students, to the instructor and to certain symbols, such as a picture of the founder of the style or a national flag. This custom, which is a way to show respect, is similar to shaking hands with someone—it has no religious significance.

But in Western countries, with our tradition of democracy and everyone's vote being of equal weight, having to bow can sometimes stick in your craw. You're acknowledging, at least to some degree, another person's superiority. If I don't like the person I'm practicing with, I still have to bow. If I don't think the senior student coming into the *dojo* is a very good martial artist, I still have to bow. If I'm mad at my instructor for forgetting that I already paid this month's tuition, I still have to bow.

A colleague of mine, now a black belt of advanced level, once told me that the bowing almost made him quit when he was a beginner. But he learned that bowing to others as a sign of respect for rank was important to his own growth.

That, in fact, is what bowing is about. It isn't so much that you're saying a certain person is superior to you, when plainly he or she may not be. It is a sign of respect for the *rank* that another person has attained. While it can be argued that people achieve ranks they have no right to, that doesn't invalidate the rank itself. It's not up to me to decide if a fellow student is really deserving of that brown belt. My only job is to acknowledge that my fellow student has a brown belt.

If we pick and choose who deserves a bow based on our preconceived ideas, we do everyone a disservice. If you decide Jimmy's third-grade teacher doesn't deserve respect, then you make it harder for all third-grade teachers to teach.

Often, we don't have enough evidence to make a valid

judgment anyway, or we're biased. We hear only Jimmy's side of the story . . . that the teacher yelled at him for no good reason when in fact the teacher might have had a very good reason.

When we bow, we're showing that our ego, our self-opinion, isn't the only important thing. We're showing that others have value, too. If we value others, we value ourselves. If you can get rid of your defensive ego-ness, you will be able to truly stand tall, knowing that you are connected to all other humans, all of whom are worthy of respect.

At the same time, our respect for other people teaches them to respect us. After all, someday you will be a brown belt, too, and you'll appreciate having those brand-new white belts respecting that achievement.

### E x e r c i s e

For one day, treat everyone you encounter with respect, whether you think they deserve it or not. Smile and say "hello" to the grocery store clerk even if she never looks up from the cash register. Commiserate with the guy who cuts the lawn when it's 90 degrees in the shade instead of criticizing the way he left that patch of grass by the sidewalk untrimmed. In this way, you're "bowing" to people, figuratively speaking. It doesn't matter if they appreciate it. The bow is a gesture of respect to yourself as much as it is to the other person.

By the end of the day, you'll feel good about yourself in a way that yelling at the store clerk would never make you feel.

## 15

# Love your teacher

It is fashionable to thank your teacher, to express appreciation, to send a box of chocolates during the holidays—but to love your teacher? Only second graders do that.

A long time ago, the man who taught me Tae Kwon Do introduced me to *his* teacher and said, "This is Grandmaster Jung. He is your grandfather in Tae Kwon Do." I came to know Grandmaster Jung well, co-authoring a book with him, and traveling with him and a group of students to meet his family in Korea. I admired and respected him, had a sneaking affection for him. But he hadn't actually been my teacher. If Grandmaster Jung was my "grandfather" in Tae Kwon Do, I realized, then, my teacher was my "father" in Tae Kwon Do. He had taught me that I was strong and brave, that I could do anything I set my mind to. He encouraged me when I faltered, congratulated me when I succeeded and didn't give up on me when I failed. He was proud of me when I earned my black belt, and he pushed me hard because he knew I could do it. He came to my wedding and my graduation.

Of course I loved him, the way a daughter loves a father. I wanted to make him proud. I never wanted him to be disappointed in me.

This doesn't mean I thought he had all the answers to the mysteries of the universe. He didn't. He made mistakes and sometimes he said or did stupid things. That meant he was human. It meant that even with my failings, I might someday be as good a martial artist as he was.

As a teacher, I am sometimes surprised when students love me. It is an honor and in some ways a burden. I have to live up to their love, be worthy of it. That makes all of us better martial artists.

You have teachers everywhere in your life. Go ahead and open your heart to them. Love them. They deserve it—and you do, too.

### Exercise

Identify a teacher in your life, past or present, who made an impact on who you are. This might be a wise old friend who encouraged you to follow your heart, a grade-school teacher who encouraged your first attempts to draw, an older sibling who has been there for you.

Write a letter to that person—even if she's dead, or if you've lost touch and wouldn't know where to find him. Express your gratitude and love for that person and the profound influence he had on your life. If possible, give the letter to the person, but with no expectation of receiving a reply. Just tell her you wanted her to know.

## 16

# Bring only what you can carry

If the floodwaters were rising, and all you could bring with you were the few things you could carry in your arms, what would those things be? Your loved ones, of course, and the family hamster, but what else? The manuscript of the book you're writing? The photographs of you and your wife on your wedding day? The cuckoo clock you got in Bavaria when you were stationed there?

Some people would require a U-Haul for the possessions they'd absolutely have to save from the floodwaters.

The martial artist must be alert and prepared to defend himself at all times. Because he may not always have a sword strapped to his shoulders, he learns to use his bare hands and feet as weapons. He realizes that carrying too much makes him tired, distracted and unfocused, so he travels light. Traveling light also means he has fewer possessions to defend from thieves.

Possessions, in and of themselves, aren't bad. But often we spend far too much time and energy on them, at the cost of our relationships, personal goals and even enjoyment of those very possessions. If I have to work an extra job to pay for my new boat, when am I going to go fishing on it? If I want to be a writer but never have time to write because I'm too busy watching DVDs, playing computer games and showing off my new stereo equipment, won't I feel frustrated when I come to the end of my life never having accomplished something I always dreamed of doing? If I buy new stuff all the time because I like it and it feels good, but it makes my wife stay awake nights wondering how we're going to pay for it all, how long am I going to have a wife?

Beyond the basics—food, water, shelter, clothing—material possessions won't fill up the empty spaces in our souls. We may need certain possessions to do our jobs, and we may need certain objects to make our lives easier, and more pleasant, but there comes a time when we're not getting good value from the money we spend. A $50,000 car is not ten times better than a $5,000 car. It's still just transportation.

In addition to letting our material possessions—and our material wants—rule our lives, we often let other baggage interfere with our goals and dreams. Is it really possible to be a high-profile lawyer and a stay-at-home daddy at the same time? Can you really be a good father when the only time you see the kid's soccer game is when it's webcast?

Often we allow others to establish expectations for us. Your parents want you to visit once a week. Your children demand your undivided attention every afternoon. The boss wants you to put in more hours at work if you expect to get that promotion. Your spouse wants you to do more around the house; the church group needs a volunteer to deliver hot meals twice a week; your doctor says if you don't start working out three times a week, it's a heart attack for you. None of the expectations, in and of themselves, are unreasonable. Together, they could drive you nuts.

So you bring only what you can carry. You decide what's important to you and let go of the rest. Perhaps you realize you do have to work out more. Who says you have to do this alone at the gym? Maybe the kids would love to play basketball with you in the afternoon. Maybe you'd like to help the church group but you just can't deliver meals twice a week. Maybe you just say no. Maybe you team up with a friend and alternate days.

The point is, you have to make conscious decisions about what you're going to do with your life and how you're going to live. Don't be misled by the ads on TV. Don't let others pile you with baggage to haul. Bring only what you can carry.

## Exercise

If you feel overwhelmed by clutter and bills you can't pay, consider how to scale back. Talk with a financial advisor or other professional about how to get full value from your money. Remember, the Joneses next door don't have it better than you do because they bought that new speedboat. They're just deeper in debt. They're not necessarily having more fun or living a more glamorous life.

Consider the priorities in your life. Are you living in a way that reflects those priorities? If you think of yourself as family-oriented, why are you working two jobs that take you away from your family? If you're career-oriented, why do you spend all your time going on blind dates just to get your mother off your back about when you're finally going to get married? Set your own priorities, discuss them, if appropriate, with your partner, and make no apologies. Go out there and live your life, unburdened by baggage that you don't need to carry.

## 17

# Listen to wise people; remember, not all wise people sit atop mountains in Tibet

Wise people can teach you a great deal about living your life to the fullest. I have had wise university professors and wise martial arts teachers. I have had wise friends. My mother is wise, although sometimes reluctant to share her wisdom, which she calls "butting in." I have had a wise editor or two.

Wise people can help you learn to grow, but only if you're open to hearing from them. Wisdom can be found in some unlikely places. My five-year-old daughter has taught me more about courage than anyone else I have ever met.

Don't discount the source just because the person has made different choices from you. I have friends who dress up every day in suits to work for a corporate paycheck and they nonetheless know things that I can learn from. I used to work with a woman who was on her fourth marriage. While I wouldn't have turned to her for advice on how to stay happily married, she did have the name of a great manicurist.

Once, when I was at a dinner, the man seated across from me asked me what I did. I said I was a martial artist and a writer. He asked about my teacher, and I said I had learned from a local martial artist, whose teacher was a Korean grandmaster. I said I had found the experience to be life-altering. The man wanted to know if I'd gone to

Asia and lived and studied there, as if enlightenment could be attained only in certain regions of the world. When I said no, he immediately lost interest and started talking to someone else.

While I'm sure it would be romantic to talk about the years I spent studying with Buddhist monks in some remote corner of the Himalayas, learning never-before-revealed secrets, it's too bad this person couldn't appreciate that you can have a profoundly life-altering experience even in the Midwest. The idea that wisdom can be found only at the feet of sages sitting atop mountains in Tibet is just plain silly.

My martial arts teacher taught me to be brave and strong and unafraid. He taught me this in the middle of Kansas. Not all wise people sit atop mountains in Tibet.

## Exercise

Think of three or four people who have taught you—intentionally or unintentionally—something important about life. Were they traditional wise people, like teachers, or was one of them a bus driver? Consider who in your life now might offer life lessons you could learn from. If you always tune out your grandmother when she gets going on "back in my day," maybe now is the time to start listening. If you still think of your little brother as an annoying eight-year-old twerp and he's twenty-seven now, maybe it's time to invite him out for a beer and see what he has to say about life.

## 18

# Discipline is not punishment

When the instructor comes into the room, all the students courteously rise and bow to her. That's discipline. If you don't rise and bow, you have to do ten pushups, on your knuckles. That's punishment.

We tend to think of discipline and punishment as the same thing, and we tend to think both things are bad, especially when applied personally to us. But discipline is essential to success, self-esteem and happiness, whereas punishment is optional.

If you're overweight, it requires discipline to cut back on the amount you eat and to increase the amount of exercise you get in order to succeed at losing weight. If you think cutting back on calories or working out is a punishment for being fat, then you'll never succeed. No one willingly punishes themselves for long (at least, sane people don't).

In the same way, if your discipline fails one afternoon, and you eat an entire bag of potato chips, you can either punish yourself by calling yourself all sorts of names and indulging in negative thinking ("You're such a pig! How can an oinker like you ever hope to lose weight?") or you can simply look at your behavior to see how and why your discipline failed. The first option—punishing yourself for your lapse—may make you feel better in the sense that now you've been punished for your misbehavior, but it isn't very constructive. The second option will actually help you to succeed. Maybe you need to keep potato chips out of the house entirely. Maybe you need one cheat day a week. Maybe you eat when you're stressed and if you can learn to de-stress in healthier ways, you won't scarf down entire bags of chips at one sitting

Occasionally, punishment is required to maintain discipline. If your child calls you a bad name, and you demand an apology, which your child refuses to give, a few minutes of timeout (punishment) might be indicated. Punishment should never include hitting or physically hurting another person, as should go without saying.

Discipline makes you feel good. "I had the discipline to read the entire chapter before class," is an accomplishment, a success. "I have the discipline to work out four times a week," makes you feel good about yourself and is good for your body. Don't confuse discipline with punishment. Work to acquire discipline. Try to avoid punishment.

## Exercise

Separate the idea of discipline and punishment in your mind. Remember, you might reward discipline or punish a lack of it, but reward, discipline and punishment are all different things.

Rethink how you use discipline in your life. It's just a tool. It can lead to good things—but too-rigid discipline can take the joy and spontaneity out of life, too.

Identify an area in your life that you think could use more discipline. Then make a plan. Discipline is just a learned habit. Beginner students don't intuitively know that they should rise and bow when the instructor enters the room. They learn through observation and remember it through habit. Once they've learned it, remaining seated when the instructor enters is not an option. They may be in the middle of a stretch and not want to get up, but that's immaterial. They have to.

Suppose you need discipline to watch your diet. Because there are teenagers in your home, you can't banish all potato chips from your cupboards. You can, however, make a plan that will help you be more successful. You can keep all junk food in a cupboard you don't need to open to get to the brown rice. You can keep the refrigerator full of fresh fruits and veggies. Instead of spending your spare time gathered around the kitchen table, start using the living room or game room. Discipline is partially a matter of saying no to yourself, of course, but it is also partially a matter of arranging things so you don't constantly have to tell yourself no.

## 19
## "Useless" knowledge may have hidden uses

Many people who begin training in martial arts, especially if they're training primarily for self-defense reasons, don't see the purpose of forms. (If you're one of them, you're in good company—Bruce Lee didn't see the point of them either.)

Forms (called *kata* in Japanese and *poomse* or *hyung* in Korean) are basically prearranged patterns of techniques—you do certain techniques in a certain order, sort of like traditional dance. Forms look nice and they require grace and agility to do well, but they're not something you use in a street fight. ("Aha! I'm being attacked by two unarmed assailants, one coming from the front and one from behind. *Chory-o* form will surely stop them!")

This fact—that you can't use *Chory-o* form in a street fight—overlooks another important truth. By memorizing patterns of techniques, you learn how to use a series of techniques. And *that* has direct application in a street fight. You may be able to stop a mugger with a single punch, but chances are that you'll need to do more than that—you'll have to punch and kick a couple of times. By memorizing effective combinations of techniques, you respond "automatically" to an assault. You don't stand there going, "Gee, what should I do now?" Because of the variety of forms and combinations of techniques in those forms, you'll learn how to follow up your first technique.

If someone punches toward your chest, and you do a crescent block to protect yourself, *Chon-ji* form will have taught you to follow up with a reverse punch. (I'm using Korean Tae Kwon Do forms here, but the same point is relevant regardless of style, although the techniques used will be different.)

How often do we consider knowledge useless? How often do we ask, Do I need to know this? When you took geometry in high school, did you hate it and wonder why you were forced to take it since you'll never use it in real life? If you eventually went into the sciences, you may have realized this useless knowledge was useful after all, but if you majored in PR, what was the point?

The point was that without geometry, you could never have built on your knowledge base. You could never have gone into science. That you chose not to anyway isn't the point. When you're eight years old and memorizing the times table, resentfully, you can't know for certain you'll never need it. Maybe you won't. But maybe you will. And if you don't have that knowledge, then a lot of doors close for you.

Learning "useless" knowledge also trains you in a way of thinking about things. Useless knowledge can teach you habits for thinking logically, drawing conclusions, understanding how the world works.

When Brazilian slaves were banned from learning martial arts and often kept chained by their hands, they practiced martial arts moves in dances their owners thought were religious rituals. They used leg techniques because they couldn't rely on their hands being free. Thus, they invented the beautiful martial art of Capoeira, which is still practiced today to the beat of drums.

If you decided that learning all those fancy high kicks was useless, and you were going to concentrate only on boxing techniques, since you know that boxers are excellent fighters, and one day you found yourself chained to the oar, you'd be wishing you hadn't made fun of those flashy Capoeira kicks.

Exercise

Make a list of the times when "useless" knowledge came to your rescue. You were able to solve a problem or hold your own in an argument because you knew the specific gravity of water. Think of times when not knowing something affected you. You couldn't get a job because you didn't know a useless programming language, or you had to call a plumber because you didn't know how to unclog the sink yourself. Then remember to keep an open mind to the knowledge that comes your way.

## 20

# You owe your teacher more than tuition

In a market economy, we have a tendency to think of all exchanges between people as a form of barter. If you supply me with one dozen eggs, I'll give you a dollar. Or, if you'll watch my kids tonight, I'll watch yours tomorrow.

So it's not surprising that we think of our relationship with our teachers in the same way. We pay them to deliver knowledge, and assume, as long as our checks don't bounce, that that's the end of the exchange.

But you owe your teacher more than tuition. In Japanese, Korean and Chinese societies, this type of obligation was, traditionally, well understood. Some obligations are reciprocal—if my friend buys me dinner one time, I'll buy her dinner when it's her turn to celebrate.

But some obligations are impossible to repay. We know that the love and care our parents gave us can't be repaid just by our thanking them. We have an obligation to care for them when they're old and need help. We have an obligation to love and honor them throughout their lives, even if they drive us nuts.

When we have children, we don't expect them to drop everything to fulfill their obligation to us. We want them to become independent people with families, or at least pets, of their own. We don't expect monthly payments from them—$150 for suffering during childbirth, $206 for putting up with them during the teenage years.

In the same way, you have an overwhelming obligation to your teacher that paying him or her doesn't begin to cover. Paying tuition simply means the teacher can devote time to you rather than working for the insurance company to put food on the table (although, of course, many instructors have to do this in addition to teaching). Tuition is basically the entry fee. Beyond that, you must give your teacher respect and honor; you must do your best to learn what he is teaching you. You must offer your own skills when needed. The teacher may ask you to give a demonstration of what you've learned in order to attract more students to the school. This is your obligation. The teacher may ask you to help teach a class, or introduce new members to the school, or sweep the floor. These are all fair requests.

Remember, you can never repay your teacher for what you've learned. What price can you put on becoming brave and strong, confident and disciplined? You owe your teacher more than tuition.

## Exercise

Not all teaching situations are exactly like this, where a student pays a teacher to show him or her a specific skill set. But think of ways you can give back to people who have had an influence on your life. Maybe you can't repay the obligation—this is often impossible—but you can thank a teacher, establish a scholarship in her name, dedicate a building or a book to her, and try to find ways to help her in her work or make her work live on.

## 21

# Chamber your kick high even when your target is low

When you perform a kick, you "chamber" your leg by bending your knee, or lifting your leg to the cocked position. From there, you strike to the target. The chamber helps you create power.

For example, for the front kick, you lift your leg, bending your knee and then striking to the target with the ball of your foot. For the side kick, you lift your leg, bending your knee, and you pivot so that your side faces the target, then kick with the heel of your foot. Different striking styles have different ways of kicking, but all require that you start the strike with your leg in the proper chamber position.

To chamber your leg high (that is, lifting your leg high, bending your knee tightly) requires strength and flexibility. If you want to kick a high target (someone's head), you have to chamber your kick high or your foot will never reach the intended target. But you can get away with holding your leg lower when you kick to the middle (chest, abdomen, groin). And when you kick low, such as to the knee, you can get away with an even lower chamber. Your foot will still reach its intended target.

But success in life, as in martial arts, doesn't have a lot to do with how much you can get away with. A good instructor will tell you to chamber your kick high even when your target is low. This makes your kick more powerful. It also helps you practice the high chamber so that when you have to kick high, you will be able to do so. (You may argue that you would never kick someone in the head, because that's an ineffective street-fighting technique, and so you don't need to practice. But what if you were thrown to the ground? Then being able to kick high might help you keep the attacker off you.) A high chamber also confuses your opponent. If you chamber your kick high, he will expect you to kick high, so you can then strike, unblocked, a middle or low target area.

Performing a difficult technique even when you don't have to doesn't make sense to some people. They wonder, why chamber high if you're just going to kick someone's ankle? They are the same people who wonder why they're the first to get laid off, or why they never got beyond green belt. Doing the more difficult task when you don't have to is good training for when you *do* have to. The more you chamber high, the easier it is to chamber high.

Keep your expectations and standards high even when it isn't crucial. You'll know who you are and what you stand for and *that* is crucial.

E x e r c i s e

List areas in your life where you let it slide—you give less than your best effort. Maybe you don't have to do well in English class to earn your engineering degree, so you let your English class slide.

Instead, make a commitment of six weeks to improving your performance—doing better in English class even if it isn't crucial.

Walk the dog every day even if you'll still be a good dog owner if you don't. Eat a healthy diet for six weeks even though you're not overweight.

Keeping high expectations and standards (for yourself and your behavior) actually helps you maintain more control over your life and helps you prepare for the inevitable challenges that will require the best from you.

## 22

## Practice Eight Directional awareness

The principle of Eight Directional awareness states that the attacker can come at you from one of eight directions. We might call these directions north, south, east, west, northwest, northeast, southwest and southeast. Or front, back, both sides and at four angles between. In other words, attackers can be all around you. They can even be above or below you. The most insidious attackers are actually inside you.

That's why you must always be aware. You must be aware of how you feel mentally, emotionally and physically. You must be aware of what is going on around you. You must develop your instincts because sometimes the attackers aren't in plain view. They're busy plotting your downfall in the bathroom.

Eight Directional awareness is not the same as paranoia. It is simply accepting, rationally, that threats to your well-being—physical, mental, emotional, spiritual, even financial—occur all the time and you must be aware of them in order to take action against them.

Unfortunately, at the first sign of trouble most people have a tendency to hide under the bed. This is not a warrior's reaction, however. If they're after you, they'll find you under the bed. The warrior knows that. She knows that you have to face an attack, defend against it, perhaps counterattack.

When your underage kid comes home late on Friday night with beer on his breath, you can hide under the bed. Boys will be boys, you can say. Or you can face it head on. You can say, "You're underage. Drinking is illegal when you're underage, and I won't tolerate it." Or, if you're slightly more laid-back, you can say, "Son, it looks like you've had a beer or two. In the morning we'll talk about why you did and why you shouldn't."

By being aware and reacting to threats, you can often diffuse an attack before it gets really dangerous. You can see the marriage counselor before you end up in divorce court. You can find a new job before you get laid off from the old. But if you hide under the bed, all you'll be is divorced and unemployed.

### Exercise

Practice Eight Directional awareness in your relationships with other people. Make an effort to be more attentive. This does not mean you have to buy roses by the dozen or arrange exotic trips to Istanbul. It just means you should pay attention, not just to what your loved ones are saying, but to what they're not saying. When you ask your wife how her day was, listen to the answer.

Concentrate on what she says. This may require turning off the television or putting down the newspaper, but life is full of sacrifices. If all she says is, "Not bad," but she's practically in tears, your instincts should tell you that something's going on below the surface, and you should offer support, a shoulder to cry on and some Kleenex.

You should practice the same attentiveness with your children. You should know the names of their friends and the names of their teachers. You should know what their interests are, even if you don't share them. If you can't name your son's three favorite rap groups, you need to ask more questions and pay more attention. If your children know you're paying attention to them, they're less likely to seek attention elsewhere, or to settle for negative attention.

## 23

# Never lose sight of the blade

It should go without saying that the blade you should never lose sight of is your *opponent's* blade. (It also helps to know where the hell your sword is, but that's a different principle.) If you don't know where your opponent's blade is, you can't defend yourself from it. In general, this lack of knowledge will result in a serious injury (usually to you).

Of course, even if you keep your eye on the blade at all times, you can still get wounded. But at least it improves the odds that you won't.

A skilled swordfighter responds instinctively to the moves of the opponent. But no matter how skilled and experienced he becomes, he never thinks himself so good that he doesn't have to worry about where the opponent's blade is.

This translates two ways: First, always know what your competition is up to; and second, never lose sight of your own goals. They can too easily slip out of your grasp.

To go along doing your business without regard to your competition can (and probably will) doom you to failure. If everyone else is offering the Model-T in various colors, but you only sell it in black, your customers will shop elsewhere. Even if you did invent the assembly-line process.

This does not mean you should always copy what your competition is doing—it may be wrong for you. But you should at least know what your competitor is doing.

In the same way, you should never forget your long-term goals. You should have one or two, probably no more than three. You can break them down into the steps needed to attain them, but the goals themselves should always be in view.

## E x e r c i s e

Write down one or two of your long-term goals. These should be attainable through your hard work, although they might be a stretch; they should correspond to some degree to your personal gifts and where you are in your life. "Win the lottery" is not a good goal because no matter how hard you work, it's probably never going to happen, and if it does happen, it will be luck, not work, that made it happen. Focus on goals over which you can have considerable control. (For example, whether you finish college is, to a large degree, entirely up to you.)

Post your goals in places where you'll see them daily, like on the refrigerator door, or on the wall next to your computer. Every now and then, change the location of the reminders (move the list from the refrigerator to the pantry door). Otherwise, it's easy to stop registering the words. You'll see the list without really "seeing" it.

Each evening, ask yourself what you've done today to get closer to your goals. It doesn't have to be much. It can be just a phone call you made. But every day you should do at least one thing that brings you closer to your goals.

## 24

# Perform all aspects of formal courtesy

We often complain about the poor etiquette of others around us—friends talking on the cell phone at a restaurant, co-workers interrupting us when we try to speak. When others aren't courteous to us, it makes us frustrated and angry.

In response, we often behave rudely ourselves. We vent our hostility when a driver changes lanes in front of us without signaling. We raise our voices when the sales-clerk doesn't bother to say, "Thank you."

The practice of courtesy requires you to be a patient and thoughtful person even when someone is discourteous to you, even if they have hurt or annoyed you. Practicing courtesy makes you a better person—more considerate, kinder, more respectful.

Courtesy involves having respect for yourself as well

as others. Not only must you treat others with respect, but you must treat yourself with respect. Courtesy is not some antiquated form of etiquette, like keeping your elbows off the table when you eat (although that can be a good start). Courtesy is a social obligation that is the visible sign of respect. And you must treat others with respect even when you don't think they deserve it. They do.

In the *dojo,* courtesy means bowing to the senior belts and to the instructor, and to any important symbols, such as a picture of the style's founder or a national flag. Formal courtesy requires you to address senior belts formally, saying, "Mr. Smith" and "Ms. Jones" or using a title such as *sensei* to address your instructor. It means remaining silent while the teacher is speaking, and thanking your training partner at the end of class. By performing formal courtesies such as these, the *dojo* remains a tranquil place, free of anger and other distractions. Every member of the school feels valued and respected.

In the same way, performing formal courtesy outside the *dojo* can make all members of society feel valued and respected. This not only means saying "please" to your husband when you ask him to do something, it also means refraining from insisting on your rights. For instance, if you smoke, it's courtesy to refrain from smoking around non-smokers, even if it's allowed. And if you're a non-smoker at a restaurant and the people at the next table are smoking, it is courteous to simply ask the server for a different table instead of commenting in loud voices on what an obnoxious habit smoking is and coughing dramatically to prove your point.

Courtesy is maintaining your respect for others even when they're doing all they can to convince you they don't deserve it. When a salesclerk doesn't say, "Thank you," it is courteous for you to say, "Thank you," anyway. If a driver cuts you off by suddenly changing lanes, it is courteous to brake and allow him the space instead of cursing, honking the horn and tailgating. You'll be pleasantly surprised at how much more relaxed and happier *you* are when you practice courtesy under these circumstances.

## Exercise

Commit to spending one day performing formal acts of courtesy in situations that require it, even with your family and friends or people who may not expect or demand it. Further test yourself by being courteous to people who you feel don't deserve it. Consider how discourteous people might have made you feel angry and frustrated in the past, but by treating them with courtesy, you find that you feel less angry and frustrated by their behavior, because your own behavior is something to be proud of.

## 25

# See the blow coming without fear

When you're a new martial artist, you have the tendency to feel slightly (maybe greatly) fearful at the prospect of someone kicking you or throwing you. You might fear, not unrealistically, "This is going to hurt."

But as you gain experience and you get popped in the ribs a couple of times, you realize that you don't have to be fearful. You can block the strike. Even if you miss, and you do get kicked in the ribs, you'll survive and live to kick your partner in the shin.

When you see the blow coming without fear, you can defend yourself in a rational, reasonable way. Your best defense might be to run away. Your best defense might be to stand and fight. But covering your face with your hands while you quiver with fear is not a good option.

When you see a blow coming without fear, you can make and implement a reasonable plan of action. If it seems obvious that your job will be eliminated during the next round of layoffs, don't just feel sick to your stomach and think, "What will I do?" Instead, rationally and logically update your résumé, register with an employment agency, network with friends and colleagues, rein in your spending in case it takes a while to find that next job. Then, when your co-workers are panicking about their pink slips, you'll be comfortable in the knowledge that you've already responded to the blow.

### Exercise

Invent a few worst-case scenarios about your life. What if your husband said he was leaving tomorrow? What if you were diagnosed with a serious illness? Although we don't like to think about these things (some of us might obsess about them, but that's not helpful either), by spending some time considering how we could react, we can face them without fear. Or at least with less fear than if we never thought about them at all, or if we worried about them but never considered what constructive action we could take.

If your husband were to leave, would you be able to pay the rent? If you're a stay-at-home mom, do you have marketable skills?

Should you get some? Okay, maybe he'll never leave you, not in this lifetime, but what if a terrible accident occurred and he died or was seriously injured and you were responsible for holding the family together financially? Could you do it? Should you get insurance, work toward a job promotion or start setting some money aside?

If you became seriously ill, do you have health insurance that will cover much of the cost of treatment? Would it be worth it to you to pay the higher premium to get better coverage? Or set aside some money to cover a high deductible? Do you have a will? Would you regret not patching it up with your sister? By facing the strike without fearing it, we can take steps to respond in a rational way, one that will leave us in control.

## 26

## Strike without fear

Around the same time that a beginning martial artist is worried about his fellow students kicking him, he has to learn to kick his fellow students.

This creates fear, too. When you're practicing with a partner, you don't want to hurt your partner, and this fear may inhibit you. You might be afraid that you won't do the technique correctly. You might fear that your opponent will block your strike or counterattack while you're striking and can't defend yourself.

These are all valid fears. You could hurt your partner. You could do the technique incorrectly. But this should not stop you from striking.

As you grow more confident in your skills, you learn to strike without fear. You know you won't hurt your partner, you know you'll do the technique correctly, you have a plan for when your partner counterattacks while you're striking.

In other words, you have to have confidence in yourself. The only way you can develop this confidence is through practice, through *doing*. If your fears paralyze you, you can't accomplish anything. If you strike out wildly because of fear, you're dangerous to everyone, including yourself.

### E x e r c i s e

Every day, we're confronted by choices and challenges that require action. Instead of dithering about how you should solve the problem, look at the problem without fear, examine your options, choose the option or options that seem most reasonable or workable to you, then forge ahead without second-guessing yourself or wondering if you should have made a different choice. That is, *do* something. And once you've done something successfully, you'll build your confidence for the next time around.

If you've been asked to speak in front of a large group at the company's annual convention, do it. Prepare yourself, yes. Practice your speech in front of the mirror and in front of any friends who will hold still long enough to listen to it. But don't let fear and worry erode your confidence. You'll be fine. Act like you have confidence, and you will have it. Put all thoughts of failure out of your mind, and strike without fear.

# 27

# The angry mind forgets skill and discipline

How many times have you said something in the heat of anger that you later regretted? Never? More than once? Afterward, you tried to apologize and make amends, but you probably did some real damage to your relationship with your dog (or your husband or your boss).

When you're angry, you lose focus and control. You lose sight of what's important. An angry martial artist forgets skill and discipline and lashes out, often ineffectively.

This doesn't mean you can or should never get angry. It just means that anger can distract you. Anger, reined in and under control, can fuel your determination to succeed. But it can't be the only emotion that fuels you, and you can't let anger be in charge.

One martial artist I know deliberately tries to provoke his opponents (no, not very sportsmanlike, but it happens). If he can make them angry at his antics, he can easily win the match. They get distracted. They just want to kick him hard instead of focusing on the goal, which is to gain enough points to win the match.

Another martial artist always falls for this provocation. He always gets mad at the other fighter's antics. When I point out that his partner is deliberately trying to make him mad, he can only focus on two things: "He shouldn't do that" and "It just makes me mad." Of course, he shouldn't do that. There are countless things people shouldn't do and yet they do them. But focusing on the injustice of what the opponent is doing won't get you any closer to winning the match. Neither will focusing on how furious his behavior makes you. Instead of giving in to the anger, you should acknowledge it and set it aside, and continue to fight in a calm, calculated, confident way.

### Exercise

Develop strategies for defusing your anger when you get mad, especially if you're prone to having a bad temper. Acting in anger leads to bad choices. Consider ways to acknowledge and control your anger. Taking deep breaths can help calm you when you're angered. Counting to ten before responding can help. Going for a walk will get you away from the scene. Taking a few minutes to close your eyes and summon your Chi will help dispel your anger. Keeping a journal lets you express your anger without lashing out at others. At the minimum, when you find yourself angry, make yourself wait without doing or saying anything. Let the adrenaline wear off before you act.

## 28
# Never cease to study

Experienced martial artists know that continual practice is necessary to maintaining skill. They also know that they should be open to learning new ways of training and teaching, even learning new and different techniques.

This is true not only of physical skills but mental and

creative ones as well. The mind is like a muscle—it grows flaccid if you don't challenge it. It isn't necessary to study only in a career- or hobby-related area. In fact, it's best to occasionally shift gears completely and study something you've never done before.

The warrior studies what makes other people successful. He listens to what makes his friends happy and what others do when they feel afraid. Sometimes he can put the information to use in his own life. Other times, it just helps him to understand the people in his life better.

## Exercise

Pick up a book, enroll in a course, watch a documentary or listen to a radio show on a topic of interest to you—not something that necessarily pertains to your career or hobbies (although you might be quite surprised at how many fields of interest can overlap and give you creative new ways of looking at your work or your hobbies).

Every few months, make a point to pick a new topic to learn more about. Keep a file with class schedules, radio schedules, titles of books you've heard about, and consult this file whenever you're looking for something to stimulate your mind again. Let others know you're interested in learning about their hobbies. Who knows? Maybe you too can learn to love Abstract Expressionism.

## 29

# Self-consciousness prevents physical action

Every now and then, martial artists have to get up in front of a panel of judges and an audience of fellow martial artists, instructors, friends and family members, and be tested on their martial arts knowledge. They have to perform their techniques correctly, demonstrate a rank-appropriate form or two, engage in mock combat, maybe do some conditioning exercises, and answer a few questions about the martial art they're learning. They have to pass this test in order to promote from one rank to another, and eventually achieve a black belt. (And once they're black belts, they'll continue to test in order to receive higher black-belt rankings, called *dans* or degrees.)

Needless to say, the testing procedure causes considerable anxiety among students. But the vast majority of their anxiety comes not from their fear of failing, but from their fear of looking stupid or making mistakes in front of other people. This self-consciousness has actually caused otherwise talented and potentially good martial artists to drop out of the martial arts. Such people literally allow their self-consciousness to prevent them from achieving their goals.

Self-defense instructors know that self-consciousness prevents physical action in other areas, too. If you suspect you're being followed in the mall parking lot, a good response might include returning to a well-populated store, and asking for a mall security guard to accompany you to your car. Or you could phone a friend to pick you up at the front door. Or you could even call the police. But some people feel too self-conscious to do any of these things. They think they're overreacting. They're even worried about embarrassing the other person, who might, after all, not be following them. They think the security guard will consider them foolish even though the mall security guard is there precisely to walk nervous customers to their cars. Self-consciousness can prevent common-sense action.

### Exercise

Don't let self-consciousness prevent you from taking action when necessary. Speak up at the next committee meeting, join that dance class you've been meaning to try. Do one activity this week that you've wanted to do but haven't yet because of fear of embarrassing yourself. By learning to act even though you're self-conscious, you will stop being so self-conscious and will become more effective in all areas of your life.

## 30

## Keep your guard up and your elbows in

In the late rounds of a match, a fighter will often grow tired and her fighting stance will get a little sloppy. She'll drop her guard. She'll stop keeping her chin tucked. A savvy opponent will take the opportunity to let loose a flurry of blows to the body and jaw that will result in the tired fighter's defeat—even knockout.

A trainer will always emphasize the importance of keeping your guard up, but until you've been zapped in the ribs because you didn't keep your elbows in, or tapped on the jaw because you didn't keep your chin tucked and your hands up, the advice seems a little abstract. Afterward, you see that it's not theoretical at all, but practical.

We all have a tendency to relax our guard in the late rounds. We take for granted that our friends will invite us to dinner, that our spouse will always be there when we get home from work, that our dog will always come when called. We assume that because we aced the interview, the job is ours. The first half of the semester went flawlessly, so now it's time to party.

But changes come to all relationships, and just because you had a good interview or you've done well on the first part of a long project, it doesn't mean you're guaranteed success. We have to continue working hard in the late rounds. We have to continue to keep our guard up.

Instead of feeling complacent about family and career, ask yourself if you should get your guard back up. Often, just when we think everything is going perfectly, a challenge or crisis comes up and we're not prepared. No life ever remains crisis-free (it'd be boring if it did). Keep yourself alert and ready to respond.

E x e r c i s e

At the first sign of fatigue—you know you have that paper due, but you'd rather spend the evening in front of the television—

assess whether you're letting your guard down. Unless you want to know what burnout feels like, you can't always function at a high level without relaxing. But you need to do this at the right time and place. Maybe you need to finish the paper before watching television. Maybe you can write the first two pages and then relax. But make a plan for handling that late-round fatigue or you might find yourself flat on the canvas instead of holding the title belt high.

## 31

## Know where your opponent will be when the strike lands

Fighters in the ring are moving targets. They can duck a punch or sidestep a kick. So you have to anticipate your opponent's reactions even before you launch an attack.

Trapshooters know that they have to aim slightly ahead of the moving target. By the time the pellets reach the correct altitude, the target will have moved ahead. If the target shooter aims where the target is now, the pellets will miss the target.

With experience, martial artists (and trapshooters) learn to accommodate for their moving targets (although they sometimes still miss.) One of the ways to anticipate your opponent's reaction is to feint—pretend to strike to see what he will do. People tend to react the same way to an attack every time they face it. A person who steps away when you do a side kick to the chest will probably frequently step away when you do a side kick to the chest.

Even experienced fighters tend to rely on a few tried-and-true techniques. If you know your opponent will step away, you can make that away position your target (or you can turn your side kick into a roundhouse kick, which will follow your opponent as she steps away).

When you plan an action, you need to consider how the target will react—where the target will actually be when the strike lands. People frequently miscalculate this and end up missing the target entirely.

If you're saving toward a down payment for a house, and you don't anticipate that house prices will go up, you can save faithfully for five years and still miss your target.

I frequently hear people say, "I never thought he would react like that." They don't usually mean this in a good way. But if they had really considered what they knew about the person, the reaction would make sense. Admittedly it can be hard to judge how people will respond. I don't know how I'll react to any given situation half the time. But I am always surprised at people who don't even stop to think about the impact of an action they've made or are going to make. This doesn't mean you don't do something because someone else might not approve. It means knowing how they might respond and planning for it.

For example, you want to work from home two days a week during the summer so you can keep an eye on the kids. (Assume your spouse or a sitter or grandparents will be keeping an eye on them the other three workdays each week.) Your job could be done from home but no one in your company has ever worked from home before. Your boss is a conservative businessman who never had to worry about what the kids were up to. Far too many people walk into the boss's office and say, "It would be convenient for me to work from home two days a week this summer. May I do so?"

The boss says, "No," and wonders if the employee is as serious about his work as he should be.

Instead, you can anticipate possible reactions and plan for them. In this case, you can show how the boss would benefit: "If I were able to work from home two days a week—which would benefit me—I'd be able to work additional hours instead of spending those hours commuting. As a trade-off, I would also be willing to serve on the company picnic task force this year even though I previously said I would be much too busy. I have a computer at home with Internet access that I could use for this purpose, so you would not need to purchase additional technology. I will install a second phone line for business calls as soon as you give me the go-ahead. We could try it out for a few weeks to see if it works for everyone. As you know, I don't often make requests such as this, and having this opportunity is very important to me."

## Exercise

Rethink a goal you have set for yourself or an action you're about to take. Have you given adequate thought to how other people involved might react? Have you taken into consideration facts— such as, labor costs tend to go up over time—that would affect your ability to be successful? Have you adequately considered your opponent's reactions? If you lower the price of your widgets to sell more widgets, what happens when your competitor reacts by cutting their price even further?

The target moves around. Take that into consideration when you're making a plan of action, and aim for where the target will be, not where it is.

## 32

# Finish the technique

When you kick your opponent, you chamber your leg and strike. But that's not all. You don't just drop your foot when you're done. This would leave you in an excellent position for your opponent to punch you in the face. Instead, you re-chamber your leg and return to the starting position.

When you throw your opponent, you don't just grab the judo top and break her balance. You throw her, then pin and hold.

This is known as finishing the technique. It's often what separates a good, effective technique from an ineffective one.

When a fighter jabs, he immediately returns the jabbing fist to the starting position, where it guards his jaw. If he doesn't do this, the opponent can punch him on the jaw and he ends up shaking his head to make those pesky stars go away.

Finishing the technique adds power and speed to the technique. It's the difference between pushing the opponent and striking the opponent.

It takes discipline to always finish the technique, especially if you're tired or you're thinking about the next technique you're going to do or if you decide your opponent isn't very good. All of these traps can be dangerous. Every fighter has gotten taken advantage of when she was tired, has been kicked while she was thinking about her next move, and has been upset by an underestimated opponent. Good fighters don't let these things happen often.

In the same vein, fighters are trained to finish the fight. This means you don't let up when the opponent is on the ropes. You fight until knockout or until the referee stops the fight. On the street, you don't kick an attacker in the groin and wait for him to run away. A smart move would be for you to get away, if possible. But if you have to fight, you fight until the attacker *does* run away, or until he is no longer a threat, or until you can get away, or until you hear a cop yelling, "Okay, okay, break it up!"

So when you have a plan to reach a goal, you finish the plan. You may need to reconsider strategies, but you don't stop before the fight is finished.

### Exercise

Pick a goal you're having trouble meeting. Vow to finish the fight. Review your plan of action, making any necessary changes to accommodate for needed changes in tactics. For example, suppose your goal is to lose twenty pounds. That's your fight. You also have a plan to cut back on calories and exercise more often. But you're having trouble sticking to the diet and you keep abandoning the attempt. Don't convince yourself that you're a loser with no self-control. Instead, remember that you're a fighter and a fighter finds another way.

Maybe your diet is too restrictive. Maybe it requires you to fix home-cooked meals after you've just worked a twelve-hour day. Make changes that help you reach your goal. (Remember, finish the fight.) One fighter became a vegetarian and started teaching aerobics classes as a way to help her meet her weight loss goals. She doesn't mind giving up beef and chicken, which saves calories. She already gets sufficient protein from other foods. Because the aerobics classes she teaches are a paid job, she must go to class, so her motivation is high. You can be creative, too.

## 33

## Your competitor can be your partner

Martial artists practice their techniques with fellow martial artists. You learn to spar by fighting fellow students. You help each other by giving advice and critiques during and after training sessions. At the same time, you might enter a tournament and compete against this training partner. Or, even during informal sparring sessions, you try to beat your partner. At the end of the match, you're still friends (assuming you were also friends before the match started).

It is impossible to improve as a fighter without partners to help you. Your competitor can be your partner.

He can do this without meaning to, such as when you take the lead from a superior fighter, when you watch and learn what a more experienced martial artist does. But you can also make a conscious decision to partner with your competitor.

For example, as a writer, I am, generally speaking, in competition with other writers. There are only so many publishers and only so many books and articles published each year. But I have also partnered with writers who have special experience or expertise to produce books that are better than I could have managed on my own.

Many businesses have found that working together with competitors, instead of directly competing, can help each business become more profitable. Companies have found that by emphasizing teamwork rather than competition among their employees, productivity improves, and so does morale.

## Exercise

Think of an area in your life where you face competition. Is there a way you can partner with your competitors for everyone's mutual advantage? For instance, suppose you're in law school and you're in competition with every other student for grades. Can you form a study group to benefit everyone? This reinforces everyone's learning. If you're weak in one area, another student can help you understand it. If you're strong in an area, you can help the other students. Everyone wins.

## 34

## Your opponent is your teacher

A martial artist learns from other martial artists. If he drops his guard, he's going to get punched. If he presents an opening, he's going to get thrown. Because it hurts to get punched and thrown (not everyone bounces), the martial artist soon learns to keep his guard up and to close the openings.

A martial artist learns from his opponents by watching them, emulating the successful ones, even becoming a student of them. He analyzes his opponents' strategies and tactics and then uses the ones that will work for him.

This requires an open mind and a willingness to be impressed. If you see a fighter using great moves but you dismiss them as flashy and unworkable instead of trying to see how you might be able to incorporate them, you won't challenge yourself to grow and learn.

Learning from your opponents improves everyone's level of performance. If a fighter inspires you to learn a new technique, you might inspire your tournament opponent to learn a new technique, too. This is good for everyone.

You can also learn what not to do. At an annual martial arts tournament a few years ago, a male competitor noticed that all of the adult male competitors in his division used power techniques for the board-breaking competition. They would do a jump reverse kick through four boards, or something similar. He decided that there was a limit to how the judges could score competitors all doing the same type of techniques—that is, if five men each broke four boards with a jump reverse kick, how do you decide who the first-place contestant is? Sure, the one with the best technique, but at an advanced level, everyone has excellent technique (if they don't, they can't break the boards). So this competitor decided to use speed breaks instead of power breaks—that is, he would use a series of fast techniques, each striking through one board at a time. Instead of a jump reverse kick, he might do a spinning wheel kick. Instead of a punch, he might do a knife hand strike. He thought this might set him apart from the crowd. It did. He won the division. Next year, more people did speed breaks, so others learned from the competition, too.

## Exercise

Make a list of things your opponent does well that you could emulate, instead of dissing her and deciding you'd never stoop that low. If you're in competition for a job that a co-worker also has her eye on, make an argument for why the boss should hire her (don't actually make this argument in front of your boss . . . this is for your eyes only). Be painstakingly honest. Then see what you can do. If she always presents a professional image, and you know you do casual Monday, Tuesday, Wednesday and Thursday as well as Friday, then you're due for a wardrobe makeover. If her degree is from Harvard and yours is from State U, you can't fix that, but you can enroll in a graduate program or take continuing education classes to show your willingness to keep up with changes in information and technology.

## 35

# Never assume a woman is not as strong as a man

Yes, there are different kinds of strength, but I am talking about pure kick-'em-as-hard-as-you-can power. As a society, we believe that all men are stronger than all women, when if we would just use our own eyeballs for a minute, we would see how ludicrous this is. Some men are stronger than some women. Some women are stronger than some men. Some men and women are equally strong.

If you know how to use your power, that makes you even stronger. For example, in addition to lifting weights to make me stronger, I know how to punch. This makes me even more powerful, in terms of the impact of my punches, than a man who might have more muscle mass but doesn't know how to punch.

When I spar with a man who is not as strong and not as skilled as I am, I can easily defeat him. When I spar with a man who is stronger than I am, but is not as skilled as I am, I can also defeat him (depending on how much stronger he is). When I spar with a man who is both stronger and more skilled than I am, guess who's spitting out teeth when we're through? But the same holds true if I spar another woman. If she's not as strong and not as skilled, I can easily defeat her. If she's stronger but not as skilled, I can defeat her (again, depending on how much stronger she is). But if she's both stronger and more skilled, then I'm out of luck.

Which doesn't mean that some guy from Jersey City couldn't come out and clean my clock for me. It just means that men aren't physically superior to women just because they're men.

This is a surprisingly difficult concept to get across to people who don't compete or practice sports in mixed-gender groups. We accept that women have less upper body strength than men do and think that proves they're weaker. We measure strength by counting how many pushups a person can do in one minute, which is a measure of male (that is to say, upper body) strength. But I have attended aerobics classes that have made grown men weep while the women involved still have enough energy to talk about the really cute handbag they got at the mall yesterday. Women tend to have more leg strength, flexibility and aerobic endurance than men, but that's not how we measure "strength."

This principle applies to other types of strength, such as courage and emotional strength. Instead of making assumptions based on gender differences, realize that all people have different strengths and weaknesses. This is important because if you're a man and you underestimate a woman's strength, you might be the one spitting out teeth. If you're a woman and you constantly sell yourself short, you'll never achieve as much as you're capable of achieving.

# Exercise

Building physical strength can make you feel mentally and emotionally stronger and sharper. It can also help you meet your fitness goals, burn more calories and prevent diseases such as osteoporosis.

If you don't already, begin weight training twice a week. You don't need an elaborate gym full of special machines to do this. Simple dumbbells will work just fine. One day you can work your upper body and another day, your lower body. You can get more elaborate, complex and time-consuming as you go on, but keep it simple at the start. You'll be amazed after a month or so how much stronger you are and how much more easily you can accomplish your tasks of daily living.

If you're a woman, don't fall into the trap of doing one set of fifteen reps of a low weight, as is often recommended (for fear of bulking up). You won't build much muscle this way. Use more sets of fewer reps and challenge yourself with heavier weights. If you're a man, don't fall into the trap of piling as much weight as possible on the bar and then throwing it up using no control and terrible form. You don't build muscle that way (you build bulging disks).

Instead, understand how strength training works. By using proper form and only by using proper form to lift a weight, you stimulate a specific muscle to grow stronger by tearing it down and rebuilding it (because of this tear-down stage, it's important to give your muscles at least twenty-four to forty-eight hours of rest between workouts). You stimulate this teardown by working your muscles to failure (you can't lift anymore). Two or three sets of six to twelve reps, depending on your goals, will produce dramatic improvements in muscle strength. For more information, consult a certified personal trainer, or any one of a number of good books designed for the beginning weight lifter.

## 36

## Train because you are a warrior

Martial artists often "sell" the martial arts by saying that training in the martial arts can help you get in shape, lose weight, build self-confidence and learn to defend yourself. These benefits are realistic—if you train, you'll get in shape and you'll have more self-confidence. But at some point you have to stop training for the extrinsic reasons and start training because that's what warriors do. They train in the warrior arts.

They don't train to get a black belt or a job promotion or because they heard it's a great place to meet guys. The idea of training just to train is a bit odd in this goal-oriented society. (And I'm a big believer in setting goals, and reaching them.) But sometimes that's what you need to do. You take a class in art history not because it gets you closer to your degree but because well-rounded individuals know a little something about art history. You take continuing education classes even if you don't need them because a professional stays abreast of what's happening in her field.

When you do this, you learn to act even when your self-discipline fails you, even when you're in a bad mood and decide you don't care if you never earn your black belt. You can easily give up on goals, you can talk yourself out of them, saying they're too hard or promise to get back to them later. But a warrior trains regardless. A warrior trains because she is a warrior.

## Exercise

If you aren't already involved in a sport or fitness activity, get started. Choose something you've always wanted to do. When you start, remind yourself that you're going to keep your mind open and learn what you can. You're not going to worry about how skilled you might one day be. You're just going to train.

If you're already involved in a sport or fitness activity, spend a few weeks deliberately putting your goals on hold. Feel the techniques and movements. Review the basics. Train just for the joy of training, not for some ultimate goal you want to reach. On days when your energy or interest flags or when you feel you're at a plateau and making little progress, remind yourself that you're training because you are a warrior and for no other reason.

You can also apply this exercise to other learning activities. For example, if you take a class, put your energy, intelligence and enthusiasm to the task of learning as much as you can from the class, without worrying about the grade that you receive. Go beyond the stated requirements for the class, not for the purpose of impressing the teacher, but for the purpose of building your skills. If you need to read a novel for a literature class you're taking, also read about the history of the time period in which the author was writing or in which the story is set. Look up the author on the Internet and find out more about him or her. You'll be gaining knowledge because you're a warrior, not just because you want to get a good grade in the class to keep your grade-point average up.

## 37
### Strategy and tactics flow from your beliefs

Strategy and tactics—your overall plan and the techniques you use to achieve it—are, or should be, a direct result of your personal beliefs.

Most martial artists believe that they should never use their skills in a violent confrontation unless they're forced to. So they believe in non-violence. If this is your belief, then your strategy would be to avoid all possible violent confrontations. One tactic you might use would be to leave (the room, the bar, the building) at the first sign of conflict. Another tactic might be to use verbal de-escalation skills. ("I don't want to fight. If I hurt your feelings with my comments, I apologize.") If a physical attack is launched, you would use tactics to get away from the attacker or control the attacker without permanently injuring him—blocks, deflections, interceptions, re-directions, joint locks and immobilizations. Only if you (or your loved ones) were in direct danger of being seriously hurt would your tactics include damaging blows, strikes and throws intended to disable and harm the attacker.

In your daily life, how you solve problems and face challenges should also flow directly from your beliefs. For example, suppose you're divorcing your no-good, low-down, two-timing spouse. Conventional wisdom would have you stick him (her) for everything you can get. But maybe you have two kids and a firm belief that their best interests should supersede any desire you have to punish your spouse for fooling around with your best friend. Your strategy, then, would be to try to work toward as fair and amicable a settlement as possible, making sure that your children's needs (health care, education costs, time spent with both parents) will be met.

Tactics would include deciding on a fair custody arrangement that will help your children maintain a good relationship with both parents (shared custody, sole custody with ample visitation rights, etc.); agreeing to reasonable support payments; dividing assets fairly. In the short run it might be satisfying to wreck your ex-spouse's life, but such action is not congruent with your belief in your children's best interests being more important than revenge.

Remember, you have to know what your beliefs are in order to act in concert with them. Your strategy and tactics should flow from your principles and beliefs; they should reflect the essence of you.

E x e r c i s e

Determine what your beliefs are about a particular problem or challenge. Then decide on an overall strategy and specific tactics you can use to act on the problem. Suppose, for instance, that you're in an urban area with a terrible public school system. You believe that a quality education is the greatest single guarantor of success for your children. What do you do? Well, obviously, you don't send your children to terrible public schools. (I say "obviously," but apparently this isn't obvious to a lot of people.)

Perhaps your strategy would then be to send your children to private schools. Tactics would include selecting the right private school, saving money to pay for it by cutting corners on less important areas of your budget and lobbying for the use of school vouchers. Or you might decide to co-found a charter school with other parents. Or you might decide to homeschool your children. Or you might move to an area with better public schools. If you have limited resources and must send your children to terrible public schools, then at the minimum you must spend time with them each day, reading to them, helping them with their homework and tutoring them as much as you can. (No one said having beliefs would be easy—or having children, either.)

## 38

## Develop *aiki*, or impassive mind

When you allow fear and doubt to influence your decision-making and your actions, you're unlikely to make the best choices possible. Think about the last time you were panicked about something—you cut your hand on the table saw and bled all over the workshop; you overslept and had five minutes to make it across town to take the final exam in a class you needed to pass to graduate. Now imagine trying to make good, effective decisions in that state of mind.

It isn't going to happen.

*Aiki,* or impassive mind, is the warrior's best weapon. It is cultivated through conscious training. When you feel yourself becoming panicked, you deliberately rein in your emotions, do some deep breathing, and think very clearly about the next few steps you must take. Give yourself a moment to think of every consideration before acting.

Taking a few moments to calm down and choose how you will react helps you make the right choices and act in a reasonable, responsible manner.

*Aiki* is developed by deliberately putting yourself in situations of high stress, and by developing strategies for handling the stress. Martial artists often compete in tournaments for this reason. Yes, they want the glory of bringing home the trophy, but they also want to know that they can perform even under high stress (such as when five judges are watching you do your form and you forget what comes next).

### Exercise

Develop *aiki* by acknowledging fear, anger and doubt, but then setting them aside in order to make wise choices. A warrior is confident in her abilities, so fear, doubt and indecision don't plague her. She knows what she's doing and she knows she knows what she's doing.

Cultivate *aiki* by seeking out situations where you have to perform under stress, even when it'd be more comfortable not to. Accept that speaking engagement, enter the bowling tournament, challenge your boss to a round of golf. The focus isn't on winning but on developing a calm mind while under stress. Do this repeatedly until you know what *aiki* feels like and can respond calmly to almost any emergency.

# 39

# Persist and you will find indomitable spirit

Perseverance and indomitable spirit often seem at first glance to be alike, but they are different concepts. Perseverance is sustained effort. It is, in essence, a series of actions. Persevering leads to breakthroughs. Indomitable spirit, on the other hand, is an attitude. Some people call it *kokoro* or "heart" and some people call it "winning spirit" or "warrior spirit."

Indomitable spirit comes as a result of continuing to try even when you have setbacks. But more than that, it is continuing to try with the right mindset. Indomitable spirit is a manifestation of Chi, of life force, of optimism. It is the sense that the world can't get you down or keep you down for long.

But in a demanding, pressure-filled world, we too often feel down. We feel put upon and oppressed. If we fail to achieve our goals, instead of taking a deep breath and trying again, we feel certain we will always fail. Since an attitude isn't a behavior, we don't think there's a lot we can do to change it. But if we can change our behavior—that is, if we can persevere instead of giving up—we can also change our attitude.

In the *dojo,* indomitable spirit means not crying or yelling in frustration when the board doesn't break for the fifth time in a row. It means smiling while you set up to try again. It means graciously and sincerely congratulating your opponent when she wins the sparring match, again. It means accepting setbacks as inevitable and not worth too much misery. It means finding what you did right even if you didn't win the grand champion medal.

The key to having indomitable spirit is to learn how to change your behavior so that you can have a more positive mental outlook. Often this requires learning to change negative thoughts into positive thoughts. Instead of thinking, "I'll never get this," you simply say, "I will get this." Sometimes your negative attitudes persist despite attempts to turn them into positive attitudes. If this is the case, consider what you have to do to eliminate the negative attitude. For instance, a salesperson might feel unsuccessful for not meeting a monthly quota several times in a row. Indomitable spirit asks her to say, "I'm a good salesperson. This month will be different." She may need to persevere to maintain that positive outlook. Maybe she needs to take a class on marketing. Maybe with the aid of her boss she can redefine what sales success means.

Finally, indomitable spirit comes from giving yourself the best chance possible to be the best person possible. This is the essence of warrior spirit. It requires you to be willing to commit your best effort to every performance. It means maintaining a positive attitude despite setbacks, knowing that you will succeed someday.

### Exercise

Try to develop warrior spirit by changing your negative self-talk. Every time you think something like, "I'm old," counter with, "I'm young at heart." Don't deprecate yourself in conversation with others. Often we joke and say things like, "I'm a total idiot," or "I can't do math to save my life." We're simply reinforcing negative ideas about ourselves when we do this. Every time you make such a comment, stop yourself and rephrase it as a more positive comment.

When someone says, "I'll bet you're mad about not getting that promotion," don't give in to the temptation to speak negatively about yourself, your boss or the person who got promoted. Instead, say something like, "Sure, I was disappointed, but I have every intention of getting promoted next time around."

## 40

# When you get fatigued, increase the pace

When I was a nerdy, daydreaming, unathletic kid, I was forced to run track-and-field in gym class. Dutifully I plodded along the track, watching enviously as all the popular kids zoomed past me. Once, when I was running the 660, a race that seemed obscenely long to me, I remember feeling thankful on the home stretch that I was almost done. If I could just keep plodding for another minute, I'd make it. The gym teacher stood just outside the lane, shouting, "Pour it on! Give it that last kick now! Pick up the pace for the last fifty yards!" (This was long enough ago that footraces were still run in yards.)

Although I was dead tired, I always did what the teacher told me, so I dug deep, found a little extra energy and went as fast as I could . . . zooming past a couple of the popular athletic kids (who were confident they'd win even without pouring it on) . . . and beating them in the race. I don't know who was more surprised—me, the teacher, or the kids I beat.

That lesson was reinforced when I began training in martial arts. The instructor would tell us to really make the last few seconds of a fight count. That, even though we were tired and just wanted the round to end, we had to increase the pace.

A lot of competitors slack off when the finish line is in sight. They let up at the last few seconds and someone else thunders right past them. When you get near the end, when you get fatigued, that's when you pick up the pace.

In training, if you go slower and slower the more fatigued you get, then that's what you're training yourself to do. Instead, you should practice increasing your pace. This actually improves your strength and muscle endurance. Which means that if you pick up the pace when you're fatigued, it means you're ensuring that you *can*.

### Exercise

The next time you hop on the treadmill at the gym to do your thirty minutes of walking, increase the pace for the last three minutes of your workout. Really push yourself to finish hard. The more you do this, the easier it gets, so you'll have to keep pushing.

Even if you don't use a treadmill, you can find a way to practice physically pushing through your fatigue to end strong. Finish the aerobics class with energy or end the basketball scrimmage with wind sprints. Pour it on at the end.

## 41

# Act directly from will

If you build it, they will come, or so *Field of Dreams* tells us. But martial artists know that if you *will* it, it will come.

In a self-defense situation, a martial artist must respond to the threat immediately, without hesitation (the roads are full of flat squirrels that couldn't make a decision). When the blow comes, doubt, confusion and indecision will defeat you. Instead, it's important to respond directly, without second-guessing yourself and questioning which technique will work best in this situation (any action is better than none).

We often allow panic or fear to direct our actions—or more likely, to inhibit them. When we're attacked, we're often paralyzed by unproductive thoughts like, "This can't be happening to me" and "My neighbor Joe would never do this! I must be misunderstanding his intentions!"

By acting directly from will, these thoughts won't stop you. When you see a punch coming, you block it. Doesn't matter who throws it or if they intended a misdemeanor or a felony. You block the punch. You respond instinctively—from the will—to protect yourself.

In our lives, we often drown out our will with a chorus of negative thoughts. We tell ourselves we can't accomplish our intentions because we're too old or too young or we don't have enough money or we're not smart enough or we're not pretty enough or tall enough or skinny enough.

To act directly from will does not mean you ignore obstacles or act recklessly without a thought to the consequences. It means you train yourself to overcome obstacles—real obstacles, not the ones invented by your overactive imagination. It means you train yourself to act quickly and decisively as soon as you detect a threat, neither underreacting nor overreacting.

### Exercise

To train yourself to act directly from will, you have to learn to concentrate on your will, not the obstacle standing in your way. You have to listen to what your heart wants, and then ignore your mind when it tries to talk you out of it.

Make a list of three heartfelt priorities in your life. These should be the things that are the most important to you in the whole universe. Mine are family, including daughter and dogs; writing, including personal and professional projects; and martial arts. Now see how much time you devote to these three things in your daily life, as compared to every other commitment, hobby, obligation and means of entertainment that fills up your days.

If you act directly from will, you will spend most of your time and resources on the things that matter most to you without regard to what the neighbors think, whether your mother approves, and even if you've never met another person who lived like that. Just because your neighbors care passionately about crabgrass doesn't mean you have to, too.

Find your will and live accordingly.

# 42

# A physical attack should
## never surprise you

Most of us believe in some basic precepts, such as, "What goes around comes around," "You get what you deserve" and "The world operates according to the principle of cause and effect."

Nicer-minded people believe that acting in a kind and generous way to others will result in others treating them in a kind and generous way. Thus, the Golden Rule: "Do unto others as you would have them do unto you." (*Not* "he who has the gold, rules.")

Those of us living in the real world, however, know better. You can be in the wrong place at the wrong time. You can be a nice, polite person and still get hurt by a drunk driver. This does not mean you should become a mean, impolite person; it just means you have to accept that bad things happen to good people, unfair things happen to even-handed individuals and Bill Gates will probably never get what he deserves.

So you should never be surprised by a physical attack. Lack of awareness (which stems from the belief that it won't happen to you) contributes to your vulnerability, and lack of preparedness prevents an effective response.

Too often, we think a threat can only occur "out there," not in our own homes. We think physical attacks happen only in the bad part of town, not in a pleasant suburban neighborhood park. We think only crazy, drugged-out strangers cause harm, not the people we know. So we are caught unaware when an attack comes.

Being surprised by an attack prevents quick action. Department of Justice statistics show that simply yelling and drawing attention to yourself when you're under attack will drive off half of all attackers. (The other half may require more aggressive persuasion.) If you're surprised, you may hesitate too long for your action to be effective.

Being skilled in violence prevention and de-escalation can help you stop a physical attack before it starts, but you have to be aware that a situation is getting violent (through clues such as aggressive posturing and verbal harassment) before you can do something about it.

Trusting your instincts, yelling *"No!"*—these are not difficult skills to learn. But being oblivious to the potential for danger makes it difficult to respond effectively when you're under fire.

## Exercise

Not only should you practice Eight Directional awareness, you should also plan for the unexpected. This does not require being paranoid, just cautious. Decide, ahead of time, what you would do in a self-defense situation. Would you scream, bite, kick? Use mace, a whistle or a weapon? What would you do if your weapon wasn't handy or you were under the covers when the attack started and couldn't kick? How would you protect children and pets? No one has a right to tell you how you should react, or blame you if you're not able to follow through as planned or if your actions fail to prevent the attack. You're not to blame, the attacker is.

But it is up to you to prepare for physical violence. To pretend it can't happen to you is foolish in the extreme.

Once you've decided on a strategy for different scenarios, get the education you need to make it work. If you choose to use a weapon, learn how to use it and keep in practice. If you have children, discuss what they should do in a self-defense situation and what they should do if they're with you when an attack occurs. Like having a family plan in case of fire, having a family plan for a physical attack is essential.

## 43
# Strive to be the physical expression of the Way

We often think of philosophical and spiritual approaches to living as taking place mostly in our hearts and our minds.

But the martial artist also knows they take place in our bodies, too, and through our physical actions—the things that we do and the things that we leave undone.

The Way is a way of balance and moderation. We should balance work with play. But often we don't understand what balance means or what creates balance. Mental effort is not balanced by rest but by physical effort. Too often, after a long day at a desk job, we come home to a long evening in front of the television. We would feel more energetic and less stressed if we actually engaged in physical labor or exercise . . . even if we just took the dog for a walk around the block.

A person who follows the Way may appear perfectly ordinary. There's nothing spectacular about such a person. She is probably reasonably fit, insofar as any limitations allow, but isn't necessarily doing handstands in the corner. She appears calm and confident. She chooses surroundings that aren't necessarily simple and austere (which might be out of balance in another way) but that are free of clutter (except when there's a two-year-old in the house) and are comfortable. Objects have a function; that function might be to chop onions or look beautiful. In the same way, clothing and accessories are simple and functional, beautiful, but not out of balance. It shouldn't take your whole paycheck to buy a pair of shoes.

When people meet you, they should think, "I want to be like her," not "I wish I had her handbag!"

### E x e r c i s e

Physical effort balances mental effort. If your current hobbies consist of watching television and surfing the Internet, it's time to add some balance. This can easily be done by finding a new hobby. You don't have to do this new hobby every single day. Once a week might be enough. (Balance and moderation in all things.) It doesn't have to be Muay Thai kickboxing. It could be gardening. Feeling the mud squish between your fingers is a wonderful way to physically connect with the world. It can be getting a dog so you can take it for a walk every evening. Or you can play basketball with the kids or Rollerblade with them if they wouldn't find it too terribly embarrassing.

Connect with your physical self to become the physical expression of the Way.

## 44

# Hope for nothing,
# fear for nothing

The martial artist does not hope to win the fight. Nor does she fear losing the fight. Either emotion merely clouds judgment. Instead, she decides on a strategy and tactics and implements them. If the opponent is losing, she does not celebrate or relax prematurely. If the opponent is winning, she does not panic or surrender. She fights to the best of her ability until the match is concluded, striving to keep her mind free from emotions that cause uncertainty. In other words, hope is not a strategy.

When your thoughts are dominated by hopes and fears, you cannot focus on goals and plans. Beyond this, you cannot be open to what an experience might bring. If you sign up for a class hoping to meet some cute single guys and are disappointed to find that of the two men enrolled, one is sixteen and the other, eighty-two, you might drop the class or sullenly attend the sessions but find them boring and unproductive, and you might ignore the woman next to you, who might otherwise have turned out to be your best friend. Or maybe if you'd been open to it, the class would have brought you a fascinating new hobby or been a step toward a fulfilling career. But if you have preconceived ideas and expectations, none of these equally good outcomes could occur.

In the same way, you might hope, all evidence to the contrary aside, that this is the year your family will finally have a contented, bicker-free Christmas. Aunt Emma won't make rude comments about how you raise your children, you won't argue with your father about politics, Mom won't be frustrated about all the work involved in fixing such a big turkey dinner yet refusing all offers of help.

You know that's never going to happen. Accept. Cultivate feelings of detachment. You know what Aunt Emma is going to say. Don't let it set you off again.

At the same time, fearing that the aforementioned debacle will repeat itself again this year, you might pack your bags and head to Munich where you spend Christmas all by yourself while everyone else is surrounded by their loving family members.

Instead of expectations and emotions, fear and hope, you can face challenges calmly and contentedly—if you hope for nothing and fear for nothing.

### Exercise

Consider an area of your life where you feel constantly disappointed. This could be the aforementioned Christmas gathering, or it could be your love life or your career. Instead of constantly feeding your hopes and fears, try to detach yourself from those emotions. Look at the problem rationally. Can you solve it? Can you convince your father to become a liberal? Probably not. Okay. Stop trying. He knows your views, you know his; talk about NASCAR instead. If you can find a way to solve your problem by setting goals, then do so. For instance, instead of hoping that your dog will someday learn to stop jumping up on people, you can take some specific steps to train him to do otherwise. You can take him to obedience class, then enforce the training at home.

If you can't take steps to solve your problem—for instance,

you want to get married and start a family, yet you're still single and not dating anyone seriously, and you've tried dating services, personal ads and more blind dates than you'd dare to count— detach yourself from the problem. If you keep signing up for classes hoping to meet cute guys and are constantly being disappointed, then you're not really living your life. Try letting go for a bit, living without hope or fear of anything, and see how it goes. You might be surprised. You might find, as I am sure all your friends have told you, that you're suddenly meeting eligible guys all over the place. More likely, however, you'll start to enjoy your life just as it is now and realize it's not so bad. If you ever get married, great. If you don't, being single is good, too.

## 45

## If I am humble, I can never be overcome

As a society, we're not all that fond of braggarts, but at the same time, we don't appreciate the virtue of humility. It seems oddly old-fashioned to us . . . and it reminds us of those smarmy, self-righteous saints or martyrs who were eager for you to slap both of their cheeks. It makes my fingers itch just thinking about it.

But humility isn't about self-loathing. It's about finding the proper place for your ego. It's about acknowledging that we are all human together. If I'm smarter or more talented than another person, that doesn't make me a better person . . . it just makes me smarter or more talented. Big deal.

When we allow our egos to get too large and we start believing our own press, it means we have forgotten that most of what we have is a gift. (And if you think all you have you earned because you work hard, remember that the ability to work hard is also a gift.) We convince ourselves that we deserve everything. More. Even if we can't afford it or our husband objects. I work hard, we think, and I deserve it—the new car, the new boat, more power at work. But the fact is, we're not entitled to more than the next person. Period. Because you have high intelligence, do you somehow have a right to a bigger house than a person with the misfortune of being born without that gift? Because both your legs work, do you deserve a new boat more than a crippled person does? Of course not.

What we have and what we are is a result of gifts we have been given. It is true that some of us are given more gifts than others, and some of us make better use of our gifts than others. But a humble person is grateful for the gifts and passes them on whenever she can to her children, her students, her friends, her community.

When your ego is in its proper place, you can never be overcome. You have a core belief in your own self-worth and the worth of others, and you don't need to remind people of your importance every ten minutes. If someone criticizes you, you accept the criticism and take what you can from it. You don't allow the criticism to stop you. A reviewer thinks you're a terrible actor. If there is some truth to the charge—and often there is not—then do what you can to improve. But don't stop being an actor. You are humble enough to accept criticism, but that does not mean you give up on your goals.

Ego interferes with learning. If you're already convinced you know everything, you can't learn anything. A humble person is always willing to learn and to grow from what he or she has learned.

E x e r c i s e

Humility is not about being a doormat or settling for mediocrity. It's about detaching your ego from the world. It's about not equating your self-worth with how much money you make or how many degrees you've earned.

Listen to your inner voice for a week. Every time you think something along the lines of, "I work hard and I deserve"—a raise, a candy bar, a new bass boat—write down what your thoughts are and what prompted them. Notice any patterns. You may see that you think you have to reward yourself for doing every task or you won't do it. Make whatever behavior changes are needed to turn off the "I deserve" commentary. For instance, if you have to bribe yourself to go to work, maybe it's time for a new job.

Then spend a week dismissing every single "I deserve" thought you have. Replace it with, "I have so much more than I deserve" or if you can't quite buy that, then try, "I already have many gifts." You'll feel less dissatisfied and more humble, and you'll get out of the "I deserve" habit.

## 46

# You must earn the jump spinning wheel kick

Some people who take up the martial arts have incredible natural ability. (I am not one of them.) They can spin and jump and kick and punch and tumble and throw. (It should go without saying that these people are usually under twenty.)

But no one can do the jump spinning wheel kick on the first try. Every martial art has a technique (usually more than one technique) that stumps people when they first try it, and the jump spinning wheel kick is the one that Tae Kwon Do has. This seemingly simple kick is in reality a complicated maneuver that requires you to jump in the air, spin in a circle to the back, with your leg extended, striking the target with the heel of your foot.

The kick requires flexibility and speed and power and timing . . . and patience, a small degree of luck, and about ten thousand repetitions.

During this process, you land on your butt a lot. No other kick causes you to fall on your butt quite so often. It is a priceless lesson in humility.

It took me almost seven years to master the jump spinning wheel kick. (I told you I'm not a natural.) It's not like I spent every waking moment working on this technique. It's not even like I spent that many waking moments on this technique. It was simply that I'd try, and fail and try and fail and after a couple of weeks of that, I'd go to work on something else. Then I'd remember that I'd never mastered that damn kick and I'd go to work on it some more.

One day, a momentous event occurred. I did the kick. I did it right. I did it perfectly. Of course, I was alone at the time but the fact that my success was not verified by independent witnesses didn't dampen my enthusiasm any. I showed off that jump spinning wheel kick for weeks. I can't imagine that I'll ever use it on a mugger (I've got something else planned for that) but I earned that kick.

There are plenty of things like that in life. You have to earn them. You can't just put your money down and buy it or log on to the Internet and download it. You have to work at it and sweat over it. Those are the only things worth having.

You must earn the jump spinning wheel kick.

## Exercise

Acquiring a skill—from playing the banjo to becoming a chess grandmaster—won't necessarily improve your health, your career or your love life. But it will improve you. The more competent you feel, the more you take charge of your life, the less dependent you are on others, the more satisfied and happy with yourself you'll feel.

Find one skill you'd like to master, be it juggling or restoring old Corvettes, and commit to mastering it, recognizing that it will be a difficult process but ultimately a lot more satisfying than spending all your spare time at the mall.

## 47

# Meditate through physical action

Martial artists know that there are two different kinds of meditation (well, there are more than that, but we're talking about broad, general categories). There is quiet sitting meditation where you empty your mind or maybe visualize your performance. The other is meditation through physical action. A state of transcendence and calmness can occur during physical effort. Although some Buddhists do walking meditation, I'm referring to the state that occurs during *strenuous* physical effort. It's similar to the runner's high that everyone used to talk about when everyone was running. You empty your mind of thoughts and cares—you even stop thinking about how hard this physical effort is to sustain—and you feel energized and at peace.

For many of us, these are golden minutes we try to have each day. That it requires a lot of grunting and sweating is a price we're willing to pay to get there.

People who have trouble doing quiet sitting meditation find that they can do physical meditation. Engaging the physical body "distracts" you so that your mind can relax. People who try sitting meditation find that minor bodily discomfort can be irritatingly distracting. In physical meditation, the focus is on performing the physical act to the exclusion of all else. Once a certain rhythm has been achieved, the mind is free to find enlightenment, destress or just empty. The result is a feeling of serenity and acceptance that helps you feel calmer and more relaxed—and perhaps just a bit closer to enlightenment.

## Exercise

Do a difficult activity for at least thirty minutes. Jogging, aerobics, biking, kickboxing—any of these physically demanding exercises will work. Focus on doing the movements correctly rather than on how out of breath you are (unless of course you're about to pass out, in which case you should go sit down. Passing out does not lead to enlightenment).

Don't talk while you're exercising. Ignore the distractions of others. Soon, you should feel pleasantly tired. Allow your mind to empty and to drift. Enjoy it. After some time (depending on your fitness level), you'll have to come back to earth and concentrate on your body again, because now that you're tired, you have to concentrate more. (Remember Lesson 40, "When you get fatigued, increase the pace.") Feel the difference afterward. You're more relaxed, and have probably gotten more from your workout than when you spend the whole aerobics class talking about your dreadful new boss or worried about how your butt looks in those new shorts.

## 48

# The centered Self reacts to few distractions

When you're in the ring, all you see is your opponent. All you hear is the referee giving instructions. You don't hear the spectators or the cell phones ringing in the background, you don't see the popcorn vendors or the kids running up and down the bleachers. Your attention is focused on the task at hand.

A warrior focuses on what's important in her life, without worrying about unimportant distractions. At work, she chooses projects that must be done and does them. In her personal life, she spends time with her family and doesn't worry about the vacuuming that is still undone.

To achieve this type of focus, you have to be centered. You have to live a life of balance. And you have to say no. This means politely hanging up on telemarketers and shutting the door on salespeople. (Why should they get your attention when you need to spend some time soaking in a bubble bath or playing with the kids or taking the dogs for a walk?) It means understanding that someone else's problem isn't necessarily your problem. People will try to hand you their problems but you have to resist the tendency you might have to help out.

A martial artist maintains her focus by zeroing in on what she's trying to accomplish right now. If she's in the middle of a promotion test, and she's trying to break a board, she ignores that fact that all the other students are trying to do the same thing. She ignores the fact that all the other students have broken their boards and she's still trying. She just focuses on breaking the board. She doesn't allow the passage of time to distract her, or the impatient sigh of the judge to throw her off balance. She focuses.

If you're supposed to have the annual report done today, and Joe comes rushing in, all concerned because he forgot to make arrangements for the shareholder meeting next week, you don't have to drop everything to help Joe (unless of course it's your responsibility to set up the meeting or the boss asks you to). This type of distraction happens frequently and we fall for it because it's more interesting to work with Joe (he's got such nice brown eyes) than it is to finish the annual report. In the same way, I'm always amused when people send me e-mails that they've marked "urgent." Might be urgent to them, but not necessarily to me. I'll decide what's urgent.

Focusing on your goals will help you achieve them. The more you focus, the less scattered and stressed you feel. You know what you should do and you do it.

### Exercise

Prioritize your time. In the morning (or the night before), make a list of the one or two things that you *must* do at work that day. If an "emergency" comes up, ask yourself if it's really an emergency, and if it's really *your* emergency. Otherwise, firmly but politely refuse to be distracted from the task at hand. (You can always offer a few minutes of listening or a piece of advice, but limit the distraction.) After work, make a list of priorities for your personal life. What must be done or the credit union will repossess the car? What else is important to you? (Spending time with family, working on a personal goal.) Focus on doing these activities, even if it means not falling asleep in front of the television.

Meditation can help you find your center. This can be done every evening before bed to help you relax or throughout the day when you feel stressed. Simply find a quiet spot (a bathroom stall if all else fails) and close your eyes, breathe deeply and empty your mind. You can also perform physical meditation, either by taking a walk or by engaging in a more vigorous physical activity. You'll find that clearing your mind and de-stressing will help you focus on what's important and not get sidetracked.

## 49
## Play

A few months ago, I was doing a photo shoot for a book on martial arts. I had invited martial artists from about ten different styles to model techniques for the book. I had one martial artist doing a kick in front of me and was concentrating on getting all the details right and finding the best angle to take the shot. I finished with the shot and turned around and saw that all of the other martial artists, instead of standing around, were showing off different techniques to each other. More than a dozen martial artists were throwing each other, punching each other, kicking each other, yelling comments like, "Here's what I'd do if you did an axe kick!" The Kung Fu fighter was sparring the Karate guy; the kickboxing instructor was attempting a Capoeira kick under the tutelage of a kid half her age; the Tae Kwon Do practitioner was getting thrown by the Judo player. In other words, they were having an awful lot of fun.

Afterward, they thanked me for inviting them, saying it was more fun than any of them had had in a while. They were thanking me, even though they were doing me the favor by agreeing to pose as models.

Sometimes we forget to play. We forget that life isn't all serious. We try hard to reach our goals without stopping. But there should be room in every life for fun. You can't always program the fun—I doubt if I had encouraged everyone to have "fun" at the photo shoot it would have been effective. Play is spontaneous. It's a matter of seeing the possibilities in a moment. It does not have a lot to do with spending money or planning extensively. You don't have to go to an amusement park or on an expensive "fun" vacation to play. You can do it in your own backyard.

Someone who is not a martial artist wouldn't necessarily find the idea of a sparring free-for-all fun. When I was in graduate school, a friend of mine and I had a lot of fun making bad puns and quoting Renaissance dramatists at each other. An accounting major wouldn't have thought this was fun, but we did.

Develop your own sense of play. When your kid tells you a terrible "knock, knock" joke, don't groan, roll your eyes and say, "I've got better things to do." Tell a terrible joke of your own.

# Exercise

Your willingness to play can be buried under an avalanche of adult responsibilities. "I don't have time for spontaneity," you might think. On the other hand, you might spend a lot of time and money in pursuit of recreation and fun without ever actually learning to play. Play isn't about keeping score or piling up a bunch of toys in the backyard. It's a mindset, an openness to new experiences.

Next time you have the opportunity to be silly, give into it. Play. You can resume your usual dignified persona afterward. If there's an impromptu Frisbee game happening on campus, you can pick up the Frisbee when it lands at your feet and toss it back to the players even if you are professor emerita of economics.

## 50

# Know what to do next

For every Plan A you devise, you should also have a Plan B in mind for when Plan A goes horribly, terribly wrong. Your backup plan may be an elaborate strategy or it may just be an escape route. The point is, you need to know what you're going to do next.

If a mugger grabs you on the street and you kick him in the groin and he doesn't let go, now what? Unless you have an elbow strike ready to go, you're in trouble.

In martial arts, we practice what to do next all the time. We practice throwing several kicks and punches in a row. We practice different ways of entering and breaking someone's balance. We work on footwork and body shifting so that if a block we execute fails, we'll still be able to avoid getting walloped on the chin.

You should always know what you're going to do next if you succeed and what you're going to do next if you fail. Suppose you're finishing your biology degree and applying to medical schools. Maybe your record is so fabulous that no one will ever turn you down, in which case your Plan B will focus on what you'll do after you're accepted to medical school. (For example, how you'll pay for school, where your husband will find a job if you have to move out of state, and so forth.)

But if you're more borderline, or if you have to have a scholarship to be able to afford to go, your Plan B should consist of a strategy for what to do if no one accepts you. Instead of being overwhelmed by rejection, deciding you're worthless, and getting a job at McDonald's, you could think of some other better alternatives. But it's best to have these thought out ahead of time. Maybe you could work on whatever makes you borderline and apply again next year. Maybe graduate school is an option, and you can become a Ph.D instead of an M.D. Maybe an internship will earn you some good letters of recommendation. Maybe you can go into an allied health field. The world is full of possibilities. You just have to identify them.

### Exercise

Prepare a Plan B. If you're up for tenure, obviously you will do all you can to bolster your bid. If you don't get tenure, however, you will probably have to leave your teaching job, so what will you do?

Get a teaching job elsewhere? Start a different career? Sue the hell out of 'em for denying you tenure? No matter which plan you choose, you can be prepared by at least identifying the strategy you'll use.

You should also plan for success. If you do get tenure, then what? Rest on your laurels? Will you finish your career at one school, or will it be time to look for a more prestigious appointment? Will you write that controversial book you didn't dare write when your job was less secure? Know what you're going to do next.

## 51

## Be a master of the moment

Much of success in martial arts, as in life, has to do with setting goals, making plans, evaluating past performance and setting standards for future behavior.

This can sometimes distract us from the fact that life should be lived in the moment.

The martial artist is acutely aware of the moment when she is fighting another fighter in the ring, when she's performing a form in front of judges during a promotion test, when she's preparing to break a board during a demonstration. To be successful, she must be fully in the moment, neither thinking about what happened before nor worrying about what happens next.

This ability comes because she is prepared. She knows what she will do next. She's not worried about the immediate future. She recognizes that she did some things well in the past and other things not so well but she is improving. So the past is immaterial.

Some of us dwell in the past, never really moving forward. "If only," we think, "my boyfriend hadn't left me, my cat hadn't died, my parents hadn't moved the family away when I was in high school, I would be perfectly happy now."

Some of us live in the future. "When I get married," we think, "or when I get a job promotion or I can finally afford a house, I will be happy."

While it's natural to have occasional regrets about the past and to have dreams about the future, you can easily waste your life—the present—by dwelling in the past or the future. The only time you really have is the present. You're either happy or you're not. Obviously, there are events that will make you unhappy no matter how much you try to live in the present, but they don't have to make you unhappy forever.

Living in the moment has to do with focusing on what's happening right now, really living it and feeling it. It's being present with all your senses. Even if the present doesn't feel so great (you just lost your job, you walked in on your husband and your best friend spoiling your new silk sheets), you should still live in the moment. Feel the anger or grief. Don't pretend it doesn't exist. When you feel happiness and joy, don't question it. ("Why should I feel happy today? I just got fired," is a good way to squelch your feelings of happiness and joy.)

For one day (start with one hour if you're really stuck in the past or the future), live in the moment. Firmly reject thoughts about the past and the future. Think about the way the sun feels coming in through the window, the expression on your puppy's furry face when you come home from work. Feel how pinched your toes are in those shoes and how good it feels to take them off.

Keep a journal. Write for a half hour or so before bed describing what you think and feel now, not what happened today, not what you have to do tomorrow. Live in the moment.

Once your day (or hour) is done, don't revert to your old habits. Renew your commitment to living in the present moment by using focus and determination and discipline to live the life you really have.

## 52
## Speed is power

A basic principle of physics states that mass times acceleration equals force. In practical terms, this means a big, strong person who is slow might have as much power (force) as a small, light person who moves quickly (can accelerate). Often we assume that a big person or a strong person (one who has mass) is always more powerful than a fast person. This assumption is wrong. It is true that a heavy object, once it gets going, is harder to stop than a lighter object, owing to momentum, but that does not give said object more power.

In the sparring ring, this means that a heavy person, once he or she gets going (overcomes inertia) is harder to stop than a light person, but a light person doesn't have as much inertia to overcome, meaning that he or she can be faster than the heavy person. A fighter who is both big and fast will have an advantage over a competitor who is only one or the other.

Why the physics lesson? Because we often fail to recognize that speed is power.

We know that big companies that move slowly cannot compete as effectively as faster-moving companies. Speed is essential in competition. If you can get your product to market before your competitor does, you can establish a bigger market share from the beginning. If you react quickly to market changes, then you sold off your tech stocks before they became worthless. If I order a widget from you and I get it a day later (speed), I'll order from you again.

Speed is important in decision-making. If it takes you twenty minutes to decide if you want the Kraft mac 'n' cheese or the less expensive store brand, your inefficiencies mean you'll have problems managing your life. If it takes you eight hours to grocery shop once a week and equally long to choose what you're going to wear today, when are you going to work (or sleep)?

Speed makes you more efficient. It gives you power.

# Exercise

Indecisive people waste a lot of time and energy on trivial matters. They spend as much time choosing their nail polish as they do their husbands. Stop worrying about these small matters and spend your time on the bigger ones (no, no, not the meaning of life . . . I mean things like deciding when, or even if, you should have your first child. Although people have been known to take far too long deciding this, too).

For a week, vow not to be indecisive. Make a choice and stick with it. In the morning, find the first piece of clean clothing in your closet and put it on. If you have two shades of eye shadow that would go equally well with the suit, choose the one on the left. If your honey says, "Let's eat out tonight," do not embark on your usual twenty-minute digression about where you want to eat and if you're really in the mood for Chinese or if Italian would fill the bill. Name the first place that comes to mind, even if it is McDonald's. If your honey makes an objection, naturally you will be open to suggestion, but you will resist embarking on that twenty-minute digression. If he says, "No, not McDonald's," then you say "Where?" If he doesn't know, then you'll go to McDonald's. End of discussion. Two (or more) otherwise sensible, rational people can get into indecision feedback loops if they're not careful, in which a lot of conversation is made but no actual decision occurs.

Not only will this speed your decision-making process, but after a couple of trips to McDonald's, you'll start knowing your own mind and will have a definite preference the next time your honey asks if you want to eat out.

# 53

# Accept the cycle of yin-yang

The concept of yin-yang underlies much Eastern philosophy. Essentially, yin-yang expresses the idea that the universe is made up of elements that are opposing yet harmonious, and that are interdependent. For example, night is the opposite of day; and you cannot have one without the other. Hot and cold have no meaning except in relation to each other.

Yin is associated with darkness, femininity and passivity, and yang is associated with light, masculinity and activity.

The cycle of yin-yang requires you to combine opposite actions to live in balance and harmony. The martial artist knows that using both hard and soft techniques is more effective than just one or the other. She knows that direct strikes and circular throws combine to make a formidable attack. Yielding to let an attack by, then striking quickly in a counterattack is an effective strategy martial artists use.

In your life, sometimes you're in an active phase and sometimes a passive phase. Each is equally important. After you work out, you must rest. If you don't respect this cycle, then you will hurt yourself. If you're always at rest, your muscles atrophy. If you never rest, you overuse and abuse your body, injuring yourself and never allowing your muscles the time they need to grow.

As you plan your day, allow yourself time for rest and reflection as well as for physical and mental activity. If you "don't have time" for that, you're going to be forced to make time when you end up sick or injured. (You can't defy the nature of the universe. It has its ways of making you listen.)

Remember, balance and moderation are the key. Neither extreme asceticism nor overindulgence brings happiness and fulfillment. You can be too thin and you can be too rich. (Although you can never have too many dogs.)

## 54

# The master of the tea is a warrior, too

In feudal Japan, a samurai would often engage in the tea ceremony *(cha-no-yu)* before battle as a way to compose his mind and prepare for the possibility that he might not parry that sword thrust in time. The tea ceremony was also used after battle to allow the samurai to relax and refresh himself.

The tea ceremony is a ritual in which a tea master prepares tea according to specific rules using highly stylized movements. The ceremony helps the master and the participants open their minds to enlightenment and to achieve a state of calm detachment. The tea master studies for many years to learn the ritual, and is often a martial artist.

The master of the tea is a warrior, too. Not only because of his martial arts training, but also because the dedication, focus and training he undergoes to become a master is what makes a warrior, whether he ever learns to draw a sword or not. Thus, the master of the tea, like the martial arts master, is worthy of respect.

In a more practical way, it is simply a reminder that appearances are deceiving. Go beyond the superficial. Recognize that learning to become a master of the tea can take just as long and be just as difficult as learning to become a master of Karate. Also recognize that one mastery is not intrinsically more valuable than the other.

### Exercise

Instead of making quick value judgments about people you meet, respect them—and their warrior aspect—by considering what their lives demand of them. A stay-at-home mom may seem to have it easy until you consider that a toddler can make more unreasonable demands in ten minutes than your boss has made in the last six months. The janitor may seem unworthy of notice until you consider that perhaps emptying wastebaskets is just as vital as crunching data, although probably less well paid.

## 55

# Train to use more than one weapon, then use the unexpected weapon

You remember that scene in the first *Indiana Jones* movie where Harrison Ford uses his whip to defeat several attackers, and then, just when he thinks he's done, he's faced with another sword-wielding maniac? Instead of using the whip, as the audience anticipates, he takes out his revolver and shoots the maniac. The unexpectedness of the weapon is the secret to his success. Neither the sword-wielding maniac nor the audience expects it.

The martial artist trains with more than one weapon. He uses kicks and punches, knee strikes and elbow strikes, sweeps and throws. He might learn stick fighting, knife fighting and how to use a gun. He might learn traditional Karate weapons like the *nunchaku* and the *sai*. He might learn Chinese weapons like paired broadswords or the segmented staff. He might practice loud shouts to draw attention to an attack and use his fingers to gouge the eyes. The martial artist is always learning to use new weapons and new techniques. He then uses the unexpected weapon.

In the ring, the fighter might perform several side kicks in a row, lulling her opponent into defending against kicks to the body. She might then unexpectedly perform a roundhouse kick to the head that scores a point.

Train to use more than one weapon, then use the unexpected weapon.

In daily life, this means being open to always learning and being willing to try unconventional approaches to problem-solving. In other words, if you and your husband can't live together, maybe you should get a duplex instead of a divorce. Take every opportunity to think of challenges and obstacles in new ways and to consider alternative approaches to handling them.

### Exercise

Try creative problem-solving on one of your most stubborn problems. Begin by writing your problem on a sheet of paper, along with the main reasons why the problem has proved intractable. For example, suppose your problem is that you need to lose weight, and a few reasons why the problem has been intractable are: You can't seem to control portion size and you can't find the time to work out. Addressing each reason separately, make a list of at least thirty possible solutions. That's right, thirty. You don't think there could be thirty possible solutions? That's where creativity comes in. Once you get past the obvious, "Weigh my portions before serving," you'll move into less obvious and maybe more useful ideas. Maybe you can buy low-calorie frozen dinners and eat only those. (Okay, maybe not the healthiest approach, but it might work.) Maybe you can get someone else to do the cooking and serve you only the portion size you're allowed to eat. Maybe you clean all the food out of the house and buy one low-calorie meal at a time from the neighborhood deli. Maybe once you see the lengths to which you are willing to go, weighing your portions before eating them will seem much more doable.

## 56
# Accept hard training

Hard training is a staple of martial arts practice. Every now and then, the martial arts instructor will go temporarily nuts and make everyone run around the block. Twice. In the snow. Barefoot. Or you go to a special class that lasts twice as long as usual and goes at a faster pace with no breaks. Or you go to a martial arts camp where all you do all day is work out. These kinds of unusual training, which require a lot of physical stamina, build a lot of mental and emotional stamina, too. Instead of wimping out when the instructor tells you to do fifty front kicks without putting your foot down, you do the fifty front kicks. Maybe your quadriceps develops a snarl in it, but at least you did it. You now know you can do something you didn't know you could do before, and if you can do fifty front kicks without setting your foot down, it's entirely possible that you can also memorize the names of every bone in the human body in order to pass your anatomy class, although you have always had your doubts.

Hard training takes many forms. Maybe you have to memorize all the countries in the continent of Africa to pass your African history final, and you just don't want to do it. You do it anyway. That's also hard training. (It's even harder training if you do it without whining.) If the only way to deal with your aunt Bernadette is to never respond to her provoking remarks about your politics and you find it incredibly difficult to ignore her, but you do it anyway, that's hard training.

### Exercise

Hard training is any difficult process we don't think we can do but that we do anyway. Succeeding makes us stronger mentally, emotionally and physically. Look for opportunities to do hard training in your life. If you find it hard to go work out after a grueling day at home with the kids, do it anyway.

If you find it hard to admit you were wrong when you started that argument about Jet Li being hotter than Jackie Chan, admit it and move on.

## 57
## Physical effort transforms the mind and spirit

The martial artist doesn't train just because it helps her keep those love handles under control. She doesn't train just because she wants to be able to fend off an attacker one day. She trains because of the mental and spiritual effects of training. One martial artist says simply, "When I train, I feel closer to God."

Probably this comes from being able to empty her mind of everyday problems and concerns and focus instead on how happy and open she feels as she works out.

Others point out that their physical efforts empower them. They feel less afraid and more confident. They also feel mentally sharper when they work out, as their overall energy level increases. The relationship between mind, body and spirit is like a tripod. If one leg is shorter or longer than the others (or missing altogether), the tripod is unbalanced and tips over. Thus, physical effort is a necessary part of a balanced, centered life. It doesn't have to be martial arts, although that's always been my recommendation. It can be any physical activity you do on a regular basis.

## Exercise

Keep a training diary, but instead of recording how many front kicks you did or how many times you lifted 200 pounds on the leg press, record your thoughts and feelings about your training. (Okay, you can also write down how many reps you did on the leg press.) Jot down your experiences: "Class was hard, but I felt exhilarated afterward" and "I couldn't do the stretches as well as I wanted, but I think that's because I felt distracted by all the deadlines I have at work. Maybe next time I should spend a few more minutes relaxing before class so I can concentrate on what I'm doing." Even if they seem silly or odd or not like you, honestly express your thoughts and emotions. I swear I have entries in my training diary that say things like, "Today, I did class and afterward felt completely at one with the universe." In a year or two, you'll enjoy looking back at your experiences and seeing how you've progressed mentally, emotionally and spiritually through your participation in a physical activity.

## 58

# Do not let the attacker set the rules of engagement

Too often, an attack goes something like this: Rapist grabs woman as she's walking to her car in the mall parking lot. Woman is surprised and doesn't know what to do. Rapist drags her to waiting vehicle, threatening to kill her if she doesn't comply. You know what happens next.

In this scenario, and many like it, the attacker gets everything his way. He sets the rules and the victim acquiesces.

In a sparring match, the same thing can happen. Competitor A performs a side kick. Competitor B blocks it. Competitor A performs a roundhouse kick. Competitor B blocks it. Competitor A performs a punch, then kicks to the head. Competitor B blocks the punch but can't deflect the kick in time. Competitor A gets a point. Competitor A has set the pace and B can only respond to what A is doing.

This is not the way to win a sparring match or defeat an attacker.

Instead, you set the rules of engagement. A man gets too close to you in the mall parking lot. You stop, say "Watch it," or move away from him. Maybe the encounter goes no further. Or maybe the attacker grabs you, you plant yourself, shout, *"No!"* and shove the attacker away, making your own escape. Maybe the attacker is a little slow on the uptake and grabs for you again. This time you unleash a series of knee strikes, kicks and punches that convince him to pick on someone his own size. You've set the rules for this encounter and you win. Now, call the police and report the attack in the hopes that the county will prosecute him and help him to a better understanding of how to treat other people.

In our daily lives, we often give up power to other people. We let them set the rules. Sometimes we say we don't care, but we should always care when decisions and actions affect us. Often the people who make these decisions are people we love and we believe they have our best interests at heart, but that is still no reason to give up power and control to another person. We say things like, "I'd love to do that but my parents/spouse/children won't like it." Of course, if you're underage, your parents are entitled to make decisions for you, and of course you need to consult with others now and then, but otherwise, you need to set your own rules.

### Exercise

Take note of how often you defer to other people or put off making a decision until you can consult with someone else. Then make a deliberate effort to take some of that power back by daring to make your own choices and your own decisions, even if they're wrong. At work, if you usually let your boss set your schedule for the day, beat her to it. Set your own schedule and let her know what it is. Of course, you will consider and appreciate her input, but you'll make the major decisions about how you'll spend your time. If your best buddy calls up and says, "Want to do something this weekend?" say, "Yes," and then also decide what you want to do: "There's a new Jet Li flick playing; let's go to the seven P.M. show."

## 59
### Don't always keep score

Fighters tend to be competitive people. They compete against themselves, they compete against others, they compete against an abstract standard they've set for themselves. How well you compete is measured by keeping score. If you could do fifty crunches in a minute yesterday, then by gum you'd better be able to do fifty-five crunches today.

If you score three unblocked kicks on your partner, who only scores two on you, you win. If you set a goal of incorporating more spinning kicks into your sparring, then you darn well better have done some during the last sparring session.

But sometimes it's just a lot of fun to compete without keeping score. Sometimes it's a joy and a delight to simply spar with your best effort and not count the number of unblocked kicks. Most warriors know that you don't always have to keep score.

If you're a competitive person, you probably have lots of ways you keep score. You count the number of degrees you have or the amount of money you make. The more toys you have, the closer you are to winning, right? But, of course, none of these measures really say if you're a good person or not, or whether you're happy or miserable. The score just tells you what the score is. It doesn't mean one person is somehow better than another, except in a particular area being measured on a particular day.

## Exercise

Think of the ways you keep score in your life. Who are you competing against? Does it matter? Do you really need to continue keeping count, or will it help the family budget if you stopped buying everything you see just to keep up with the neighbors? Do you keep track of what other people "owe" you? If someone owes you a favor, do you resent doing one for them until they "pay up"? Maybe you need to stop keeping score.

## 60
# Losing teaches more than winning

Although I personally much prefer winning to losing, I have found that I learn far more lessons from losing than from winning. When I win, mostly I learn things like, "Ah! This feels good." But I probably didn't have to win to be able to anticipate that I'd like it. I could have guessed that ahead of time without having to win at all.

When I lose, that's when I test my true character. I find out if I really am a good sport. I learn not to underestimate scrawny green belts. I learn that sometimes when you're too aggressive, you can trip over your own feet. All of these are terrific lessons and they've helped me go on to win the next time.

In my everyday life, I learn what doesn't work a lot more than I learn what does work. But this helps me to focus on what does work. Because I don't have any special fear of losing, I don't mind taking risks. I don't mind setting high goals for myself. I figure even if I flame out in a spectacular crash-and-burn failure, at least I have learned something. And I'll have provided some entertainment to the spectators.

Mostly, though, I've found that my willingness to lose has helped me achieve much, much more than people terrified of failure, or people who say, "Failure only teaches you how to fail." A person who thinks failure is not an option won't take any meaningful risks.

I was overweight, out of shape and totally unathletic when I began training in martial arts. If I had failed at that endeavor, how would I be worse off? I would still be overweight, out of shape and unathletic. Big deal. I already was that. If there were eight other overweight, out of shape and totally unathletic people who never tried martial arts, how would my trying and failing make me worse off than they were? I wouldn't be.

But instead I succeeded against most predictions and found a new, rewarding way of life that led directly to a career I'd always dreamed of. Those eight other people are still overweight, out of shape and unathletic, telling themselves that failure is not an option.

Think of the last time you lost at something. It doesn't have to be especially significant, but it probably needs to be a little more important than losing at checkers to your grandfather (although it's possible you learned something from this experience). Consider what you learned from losing other than the fact that you don't like losing. Then consider how you have applied (or can apply) those lessons to your life. See? Losing's not so bad after all.

## 61

## No one fails who keeps trying

If an attacker grabs you on the street and you yell, "No! Let me go!" and the attacker doesn't let go, have you failed at defending yourself? Of course not. There's plenty left you can do to make the attacker let you go.

If you're trying to break a board with a side kick, and you kick the board, and it does not break, have you failed to break the board? Not if you kick it again. (You may have failed to break the board on the first try, but that is not the same thing, and it's not the most important thing.)

It's saddening the number of people who try something once and fail and consider themselves failures. I know would-be writers who get two or three rejection letters and give up because they're failures. I might be dense, but in the course of my writing career, including the days before I was published, I have received literally hundreds (maybe thousands) of rejection letters. But I've published almost twenty books. That's not failure. So if getting a thousand rejection letters isn't failure, how can getting two or three be failure? I always assumed that I was in fact a talented, maybe even brilliant, writer, but that my timing was off or that I was just asking the wrong editors—for instance, the ones who couldn't perceive my brilliance. So it just never occurred to me that I had failed. I just wasn't successful at that time.

I admit that my confidence was shaken now and then by the sheer weight of that avalanche of rejection but I knew I would keep trying until I was dead, after which time it presumably wouldn't matter to me if I had ever gotten published or not. I don't know that I would have continued persisting, however, if I had not had martial arts training.

In all martial arts, perseverance is a key component to success. If you can't do the side kick on the first try, you just keep trying it until you can do it. You're not a failure because you can't do the kick on the first try or the tenth try. You're not a failure if you can't do the kick even though the person next to you who started at the same time can. You're just a learner, still trying. You just haven't succeeded yet.

### Exercise

If you have a goal that you've given up trying to reach, re-examine it. Do you really want to abandon the goal? Is it really no longer worthwhile to you or have you just given up hope that you'd achieve it? Dust off the goal and give it another try—or another dozen tries. As long as you're trying, you haven't failed. (These

have to be meaningful tries, not half-hearted attempts, or there's
no reason to bother.)

## 62

# If you think you don't have enough, you will never have enough

The *Tao Te Ching* teaches us how to find *Tao* (the Way).
But our progress along the Way is often interrupted or entirely derailed by distractions. One of these distractions is
wanting.

The *Tao Te Ching* tells us, "If you think you don't have
enough, then you will never have enough." With the exception of someone who is homeless and starving (and if
you've just bought this book, you're not that someone),
we all have enough. Most of us don't see it that way. Instead, we see what we lack. We think, if only we owned a
bigger house or a fancier car, if our hair was blonde or we
weighed twenty pounds less . . . then, *then* we would be
happy.

But, of course, we wouldn't be. Feeding our wants
doesn't fill up that big ole hole. It just makes the big ole
hole bigger. If the ice cream cone didn't satisfy us, then
maybe we need the double chocolate sundae. And if the
sundae doesn't fill us up, then it's time to graduate to the
banana split. At what point do you stop? After you've
bought the ice cream factory? Instead of meeting our
needs and being happy to have a few luxuries, we let our
wants take control.

If you think you don't have enough, you will never have enough.

## Exercise

When the "I wannas" strike, you should counter them with logic and reason, even though the "wants" are primarily emotional. The reason this works is because we try to convince ourselves that we "need" something that we "want." By looking at the "want" logically, we see it for what it is: a want. If you think a membership at the country club will make you happy, ask yourself why. The answer is, it can't make you happy. It might give you something to do on the weekends, but if your problem is that you're bored, you can probably find solutions to that problem that don't require you to take out a bank loan.

By being objective, you can separate your wants from your needs. By focusing on your needs for love, meaningful work and good relationships, you'll drastically reduce the number of wants you have.

# 63
# We're all teachers and we're all students

Martial artists teach each other formally and informally. They help each other out, show each other new moves, critique each other's techniques.

When you're a beginner, you soak up information. You're paired with people who know more than you do and people who know less than you do. You learn from the people who know more than you do and you teach the people who know less than you do.

Eventually, you become an instructor and, while you're teaching, your students also teach you. They make you learn why the techniques are done a certain way (because they ask why). They push you to learn more difficult techniques because they want you to show the techniques to them. They teach you how to find thirty-six different ways of saying the same thing.

In our lives, we often take one role or the other, positioning ourselves as either the expert or the untutored. But we should really be both. We should teach others but also be willing to learn from them. The teacher and the learner are one and the same.

## Exercise

We often emphasize being open to learning and being a lifelong learner, but we don't often emphasize the corollary, which is to be a teacher. Each of us has knowledge that can be useful to others. Share this knowledge. Offer to teach your niece how to bake. Sign up to teach an adult education class in ceramics. Agree to be an online tutor for your kid's school. Give yourself opportunities to hone your teaching skills (even if getting up in front of the class makes you nervous!). Not all teaching has to be done in a formal setting in front of a couple dozen dues-paying students. Sometimes it can be informal, one-on-one sessions. Either way, you will learn as much (probably more) from the experience of teaching as you will learn by being a student, no matter how diligent.

# 64

# A kick must be repeated 10,000 times before you know how to do it

If I had known that a kick must be repeated 10,000 times before you know how to do it, I would probably have walked right on by that Tae Kwon Do school and signed up for aerobics at the gym down the street. Who knew knowledge could be so hard? Or so time-consuming?

A beginner is often thrilled to see that after a few tries, he is able to do the kick. But being able to do the kick and mastering the kick are two different things. And many martial artists argue that you never do truly master any technique . . . you just become very, very good at it, although you could conceivably always become better at it.

Physiologists point out that to train a muscle to perform a specific movement correctly, without your thinking about it, requires thousands of repetitions. That's why all those cute babies stagger around for months after they've taken their first step. They know how to walk. They just haven't mastered it yet.

The mastery comes when you can perform the technique without thinking and you can do it correctly, effortlessly and consistently. Often, you're a black belt before this happens and often, when you're a black belt, you see that you're still just a beginner in many ways. You are just beginning your mastery.

If it takes 10,000 repetitions to learn the side kick—and that means 10,000 as-perfect-as-possible repetitions, otherwise you're just training your body in how to do a sloppy kick—then the key to mastery is practice.

Studies have shown that masters of any activity, athletes and pianists alike, share one thing in common: They practice significantly more than people who are merely good or competent at what they do. The virtuoso pianist practices the scale 10,000 times, just as the martial arts master practices a kick 10,000 times.

Exercise

Practice is necessary to mastery. But often we underestimate how much practice is needed, and we overestimate how much practice we do. Any skill that you want to master requires daily attention, sometimes hours of practice each day. That requires true commitment.

Choose a skill you've always wanted to master. It helps to start with something small, like learning to use chopsticks. Set aside time in your schedule each day to learning to manipulate the chopsticks. Setting aside all day Saturday won't do it. You need the daily practice. Soon you'll know how to use chopsticks and can progress to more difficult skills. Learning how to master one skill, no matter how small, teaches you how to master others and encourages you to devote sufficient practice time to the process.

## 65

# If you don't fall down now and then, you're not trying hard enough

Every martial artist, attempting a new throw or trying an unfamiliar kick, occasionally ends up falling down, although this is not his goal. When you challenge yourself by setting the bar higher, you can whack your hip on the bar.

This does not mean that you should immediately lower the bar or that you should fear whacking your hip and never raise the bar. It means that if you do whack your hip, you're trying. If you never whack your hip, you're not trying hard enough.

Every martial arts instructor has a student or two (or ten) who never stretch themselves. They never try to do anything if they're not sure they can do it. Sometimes they laugh at the people who do try, and who whack their hips. Fortunately, these students either learn to try or they stop coming.

Don't let the fear of someone laughing at you stop you from trying and from challenging yourself. Those people who laugh are too afraid to try themselves. They use your whacking your hip as a further excuse not to try themselves.

But not everyone is laughing at you. Only the ignorant are, and who cares what they laugh at? They'll never learn new skills or master a body of knowledge. In fact, most of the time, no one really notices you whacking your hip. You just think they do. If they do notice, they understand that you're trying. Usually they don't go home and post it all over the Internet: "Ann raises the bar and whacks her hip."

We often reach certain comfort levels in our lives. We feel that things may have gotten monotonous, and the phrase "stuck in a rut" has a certain applicability to our situation, but it's comfortable here. Everything works okay. No one's whacking their hips or banging their shins.

They should be. Life is a journey of learning and growing, not sitting in front of the television like a lump. If your life has become too comfortable and you're too complacent, it's time to raise the bar.

## Exercise

Getting out of your comfort zone can be quite painful. You like it there, otherwise you wouldn't be there. But at some level, you know it's not right, it's not the best way to live. So do something to shake up your life. This semester, set your sights on getting all A's instead of settling for the B's that you can get without working so hard. Maybe you don't "need" to get all A's—you'll still get a job after college if you don't—but that's not the point. Plenty of people will try to encourage you to settle for mediocrity. They'll ask you to go for a beer when they know you have to study. They'll tell you grades don't matter, so you can let it slide this time. But that just encourages you to get in the habit of mediocrity.

Suppose you set your sights on all A's and you fail. You get four A's and two B's. You fell down, so to speak. Whacked your hip on the bar. Even so, you're doing much better than last semester, when you got six B's. And you're teaching yourself how to strive and how to achieve. If you don't fall down now and then, you're not trying hard enough.

## 66

# To jump, both feet must leave the ground

I tell this story all the time: When I was learning to do a jump reverse kick, I was taught that you jump up, spin to the back and kick the target with the heel of the foot that started farthest from the target. This kick is taught at the intermediate level, so even fairly new martial artists can learn how to do it.

Not me.

This is a powerful kick, and you could drop even a big attacker with it. But I was always afraid of that jump. I thought I might fall. Or I might land wrong. So I did the kick with one foot on the ground. During promotion tests, I would break boards with my version of the jump reverse kick. It was a powerful kick, even if I was doing it wrong. I used it in sparring, and I congratulated myself on having such a good quasi-jump reverse kick.

One day, the instructor had everyone in the class pair up. One partner held a kicking target while the other practiced jump reverse kicks. The instructor held the bag for me. I kicked it. I kicked it hard. He said, "Your feet are supposed to leave the ground when you do this kick."

"I know," I said. "Sir. But—"

"Both feet are supposed to leave the ground," he said, and waited.

So I took a deep breath, and I crouched low, and I

sprang three, maybe four, inches off the ground and I did the kick. I didn't fall over, which was a relief.

"There," the instructor said, handing the target back to me. "That's how you do it."

Well, I knew you were supposed to spring more than three inches off the ground, but I understood what he meant. For the first time, I had done the kick correctly, with both feet off the ground.

Our fears stop us every day from doing things we want to do. Our fears stop us from taking risks. We're afraid we'll fall down.

But life sometimes requires us to take risks. We can stay in a job we hate or we can risk looking for a new job. We can start our own company, or let all our talents and creativity be used to enrich others. We can risk dating again or stay home wishing we had some companionship.

Sometimes the risks and rewards are less obvious. Maybe you've always wanted to own a cat but are afraid you won't be able to train it to use the kitty litter successfully. Probably your life will manage to lurch along even if you never adopt a cat. So taking the risk is not imperative.

Even when the risk is not imperative, it should sometimes be taken. Surely my jumping with both feet has not altered the course of human history. But it certainly has changed how I feel about my abilities. I can jump with both feet off the ground . . . what else can I do that I didn't know I could?

Not all risks are worth taking, obviously. Sometimes the results, should you fail, are too serious. If starting a company that subsequently fails would bankrupt you, your parents, both your sisters and three of your closest friends, you might think about getting a job instead (or you might think of starting your company in such a way that your failure wouldn't ruin so many people). But rarely do the risks of failure so far outweigh the possible rewards of success.

If I had failed graduate school, would that have been the end of the road for me? If I had failed to earn my black belt, would I be unemployable? Of course not. In either case, I would have learned some useful skills and knowledge even if I ultimately failed or abandoned the attempt.

### Exercise

Practice risk-taking. This does not mean bungee-jumping off bridges, driving drunk or having unprotected sex. (You should know that, but I felt it prudent to make a disclaimer.)

Go ahead and become a platinum blonde if you've been aching to try for three years now. Adopt that new puppy, paint the walls purple, take that Reiki energy workshop even though you're not entirely sure what that is. Find one risk this week and take it. Enjoy the experience. Now find another risk. Jump with both feet off the ground and see what happens.

## 67

# Anticipate your opponent's moves

Two fighters circle each other, feinting and jabbing, feeling each other out without committing to a full-fledged attack. Each fighter wants to know what the other fighter is going to do. If Fighter A does a roundhouse kick, will Fighter B counter with a reverse kick to A's unguarded midsection? Can Fighter A, anticipating this, block the reverse kick in time? What if Fighter B doesn't use a reverse kick at all?

Ah, the problems you have to solve when you're sparring. Usually you do the problem-solving intuitively. Experience and training teach you to anticipate the reverse kick but to keep your head guarded just in case she uses a spinning wheel kick instead of a reverse kick as a counter.

You can anticipate your opponent's moves in several ways. First, there are a limited number of possible responses to the roundhouse kick. You can block it. You can do a reverse kick. You can do a spinning wheel kick or a spinning backfist. Pretty much anything else will be ineffective. An experienced fighter knows this and plans accordingly. Second, you can test your opponent by feinting. You start a roundhouse kick but don't complete it. Your opponent, on seeing you start the kick, will respond with a countering technique. Since you're not committed to the kick, you can see what the counter is and respond to the counter. The next time you do the roundhouse kick, you'll have a good idea of how your opponent will respond.

Third, you can anticipate your opponent by sparring with him or her frequently. People do not change their strategies and tactics very often. If your partner is a defensive fighter who always waits for your attack before counter-attacking, your partner will always be a defensive fighter—for this match and the next six. Yes, it would be wise to change strategy, but few fighters ever do. You can use this knowledge to your benefit.

How do these guidelines apply outside the ring? To anticipate your opponent/competitor, you have to:

1. Know your business.
2. Test your competitor.
3. Know your competitor.

One approach is not enough. You have to combine all three to truly be able to anticipate your opponent's actions. Even then, you might get the occasional surprise, but the more you're able to plan for what the competition will do, the more likely you will win the match.

### Exercise

A nice person like you doesn't have opponents, right? This lesson can apply to any situation where we have different goals from another person, or where the goals of two or more people conflict. If you can anticipate the other person's actions and reactions, you have a better chance of success.

The next time such a conflict looks as if it will surface in your life, prepare for it as a warrior does. For instance, suppose you decide that you need more help around the house and you have two teenagers who are perfectly capable of doing more chores than they're doing. If you simply tell them they have to do more chores, you can readily anticipate that they'll complain and possibly that they'll ignore the command and might not do it. This means they "win." In order for you to win, you need to plan for this reaction. Consider what your options are. You're not likely to boot them out of the house if they don't comply, so that's not a technique in your arsenal that you can use effectively in this situation. What are your other alternatives? You can operate on a punishment basis: If they don't help out, they don't get the keys to the car on Friday night. You can operate on a reward basis: If they do help out, you'll raise their allowance, buy them the skateboard they've had their eye on or chauffeur them to their friends' houses twice a week. You can get creative: If they'll contribute money from their part-time job, you'll hire a housekeeper. If they don't want to do that, then they'll have to do their assigned chores.

Of course, you also have to test your techniques. If one technique doesn't work, try another. Don't give up and do all the laundry yourself. Remember that just as a warrior may have to use more than one technique to defeat an opponent, you may have to use more than one technique to resolve a problem.

The next time your goals (or wants or needs) seem likely to conflict with someone else's, anticipate how they will act and prepare for it.

## 68

# Don't telegraph your moves

A good fighter can anticipate what his opponent is going to do just by watching him. A fighter who's about to do a front leg kick will suddenly shift his weight to his back leg. A fighter about to do a reverse kick will bring his back shoulder slightly forward to "wind up" for the spin. A fighter about to kick to the solar plexus will glance at the target area just before unleashing the blow. All these clues are giveaways to the trained fighter. A person who telegraphs his front leg kick will find the front leg kick blocked.

Obviously, it's not wise to telegraph your moves. If you do, your opponent can block them and counter them, scoring points on you (wasn't it supposed to be the other way around?).

In our daily lives, we have a tendency to talk about our plans, dreams and goals to anyone who will hold still long enough to listen. In general, this doesn't hurt us (just as in sparring, where sometimes telegraphing your moves doesn't hurt because your opponent is inexperienced or you're incredibly fast).

But sometimes this tendency to tell all does hurt us. How? A few ways. First, you can be harmed through sheer malice. You tell everyone that you're going to buy that gorgeous dress in the window at Sak's. They have one size eight left—just your size! And it fits like a dream. So someone who has a little malice in her heart might go and buy the dress before you do. Oops. Shoulda kept your mouth shut.

Second, it allows others to act before you're ready. More and more companies are terminating employees as soon as they find out said employees are looking for other jobs. It's also common for a person who has politely given notice to be told, "Leave today." If you needed that two weeks' pay, sorry. If you were looking for but hadn't found a job and got your pink slip, now you're in trouble. Although you know networking can help you find a new job, you also have to realize that word can get back to your boss and you might lose your old job.

Third, people can discourage you. When I decided to go to graduate school, I announced my decision to some people who laughed at me. Apparently, I was too stupid to earn a Ph.D. (Someone should tell the committee that awarded me the Ph.D.) If I hadn't already quit my job, their lack of belief and discouragement would probably have made me reconsider my choice. Yet graduate school was one of the best things I've ever done for myself.

Of course, there will be times when you need to consult with others before you make a move. But you should always play it close to your vest. Consider your life to operate on a need-to-know basis. Who needed to be in on my decision to go to graduate school? Since I was single and paying for it myself, no one needed to know. Except, of course, the graduate school. I would have been better off keeping my plans to myself instead of opening myself up to fear and doubts planted by others.

Next time you're all set to tell your plans to the person in the cubicle next door, stop. Ask yourself what you'll gain by telegraphing your moves. If it's something good, then go ahead and tell the world. If you're having a party and everyone's invited, go ahead and tell the world. But if only a few worthy individuals are invited, keep your mouth shut or you'll cause hurt feelings.

## 69

## Keep your eye on the Way, not the destination

Death is ultimately the end, or destination, of each of our lives. But death is not what gives meaning to our lives. The journey gives meaning. Keeping the destination—death—ever-present in our minds can only cause us to miss out on much of the joy of life. Yes, we know that death is out there, and we take steps to prevent our prematurely reaching that destination, but it doesn't, or shouldn't, preoccupy us at all times.

A beginning martial artist knows that the black belt is the destination. He also knows that the journey doesn't end once that destination has been reached. It changes, of course. In some ways the journey is just beginning. (A person doesn't achieve a black belt and then abandon the journey.) But a beginning martial artist focused only on the destination won't enjoy the journey, won't revel in the feeling of accomplishment from learning the first form, the delight you get from seeing a muscle sprout when hitherto it was buried under fat.

It's important to have goals and to identify the steps needed to achieve the goal. But focusing solely on the goal will rob you of a lot of pleasure.

Say your goal is to write a book and have it published. You have identified steps needed to reach that goal. You set aside time to write every day and after a couple of months, you've got a good book finished. So you send it off to a publisher, who rejects it. Ruins your whole day, doesn't it? Makes you want to abandon the attempt, right?

It shouldn't. The goal is just a goal. The journey is the important thing. You got up today—that's a plus. Your kid gave you a hug—that's a joy. Are you going to let a rejection letter rob you of that pleasure? Of course not. You know that there are other publishers out there. You know that even if none of them ever publish your book, writing it was a pleasure. And you've learned something about the publishing industry, so maybe next time you'll have a better chance of succeeding. Maybe you've met other writers who you enjoy having in your life. Maybe you went to a writers' conference in a part of the country you had never seen before. These parts of the journey may have been interesting, stimulating and fun.

Enjoy the journey. It should be meaningful. It is the only one you will ever have.

## Exercise

Look at your goals. Know them. Then focus on what you're doing to get there. If you want to achieve black belt, fine, but focus on learning the techniques you're being taught as a white belt. Enjoy the beginner stage. Don't hope you can accomplish the journey faster (a black belt achieved in six months would be worthless anyway.) Don't get frustrated when you hit a plateau and don't appear to be making progress. Just keep training. It will come.

Being goal-oriented is good, even admirable, but it can cause you to miss some good things along the way. Know what your goals are but don't let them make you lose sight of the journey.

## 70

## Patience

Mastery takes time. It takes practice and commitment and effort, but it also takes time. Often during that time, you just have to be patient. It will come. When you're a martial artist, as you learn the techniques, you can get frustrated because you can't figure out how to do a certain kick correctly. You practice and practice and it doesn't come. Instead of giving up, just be patient. If you can't do the kick even though you've tried repeatedly, turn your attention to another technique for a while. Then return to the kick that was giving you trouble and try again.

Often martial artists reach a plateau when they're advanced-intermediate practitioners. They're not beginners, and they've been intermediate-level students for a while but are not yet black belts. They feel that nothing is getting better. This is the nature of physical and mental learning. A child learns so much in the first three years of life that it is literally unbelievable. Then learning slows. The beginning martial artist learns many new techniques in the first months of learning. But after a while learning slows. There aren't so many techniques to learn. Now the problem is to master them. That's a slow process.

The martial artist may feel his sparring isn't getting better and his forms aren't improving. He still always gets third place at tournaments. Maybe it's time to take up golf.

Patience.

The incremental improvements that are happening at this level are hard to see. Much of what takes place is mental—the martial artist begins to understand why certain techniques are done a certain way and how the body should move to do the techniques. These refinements will eventually lead to greater mastery, but usually not until after a very trying period of stagnation.

Eventually the spark comes, the next step is reached, the plateau is left behind. But not if you've already abandoned the journey.

Patience helps in all areas of life. Having a five-year-old requires more patience than anyone ever warned me. Career success requires patience. Finding the right job or the right college or the right partner requires patience. But the ability to wait will be rewarded in the end.

# Exercise

Begin exercising patience in small things. A driver cuts you off. Instead of screaming obscenities and making gestures your mama would not approve of, take a deep breath and be patient. Not everyone is as competent a driver as you are. Relax.

When it takes half an hour to navigate the phone company's voice-mail system, resist the urge to smash down the receiver. Also resist the urge to scream at the first human voice you hear. (The reason the phone company has that maze to begin with is because everyone is always yelling at the phone company reps, and they're hoping you'll give up and go away.)

Instead, register a complaint about the system and then make whatever request it was that made you call the phone company in the first place. Contrary to popular opinion, expressing your anger all the time does not help you get it out of your system. It just helps you practice it so you get better at it. Nothing wrong with being angry or expressing it in a reasonable way, but screaming and throwing things just makes you good at screaming and throwing things. Who wants to be that person? Who wants to be with that person?

Once you master being patient with the phone company, you'll be able to be patient in all things.

# 71

## Self-understanding requires self-acceptance

When I began training in martial arts, I hated my body. I had been diagnosed with rheumatoid arthritis when I was nineteen, and had gradually stopped doing all but the simplest everyday activities. I was overweight and out of shape and had just quit smoking. I wanted to start smoking again. I hated my aching, flabby body. It betrayed me all the time. Sometimes my knees just wouldn't hold me up. I'd be walking along and I'd fall down. It sucked.

When I started training, the very first lesson totally transformed my relationship with my body. Look at that! I could kick! I could punch! The instructor said I even picked it up pretty fast!

I was still overweight and out of shape. I still had rheumatoid arthritis.

After a few months of training, I learned a really cool form. Forms are patterns of movements that you memorize and practice, like a dance. Forms show your grace and agility. So, I had learned this form, and I was doing it one day, and it was flowing effortlessly, and I caught sight of myself in the mirror, and you know something? I was beautiful.

I was still overweight and out of shape. I still had rheumatoid arthritis. But I no longer hated my body. Look at all it could do! It was a magnificent body. It was beautiful.

I began to imagine that it could do more if I took better care of it. So I wanted to. I accepted my fat, unfit, aching body. Once I did, I began to understand why I treated it the way I did. I punished my body and its failures by smoking (even though I had recently quit, I was finally able to understand the addiction). If I didn't take care of my body and treat it well by eating right and exercising it, well, that was because my body didn't deserve it.

Once I began to understand the reason for my behavior, I could change it. My body wasn't the enemy after all. And if I ate right and exercised, it would have fewer problems. So that's what I started doing, and I lost weight and got strong and fit.

After my daughter was born, my life changed completely. She was in and out of hospitals with dizzying frequency. She saw a battalion of specialists. I was afraid she would die. I was afraid she wouldn't die, and that she'd be a vegetable. I had little time for training. I ate a lot. My marriage fell apart. I crawled out from under the wreckage one day, blinked, looked around and realized I had gotten overweight and out of shape again. I could have hated myself for that. But I had learned something. What I learned was that no one is superwoman. If I managed to survive the first chaotic years of my daughter's life and the end of my marriage with nothing worse to show for it than a few extra pounds, then I was doing all right. Some people turn to drink, and some to drugs. Others bury themselves in their work or slide into depression. It was a lot healthier for me and my daughter that I happened to find my comfort in chocolate cake.

Didn't mean it was okay to continue in this vein. Just meant I forgave myself for what had happened. It was okay. It happened. It could have been worse.

I knew, you see, that my body was still beautiful. I began weight training to help me get back in shape, and I was delighted to see how strong I still was. Even though I was fat and out of shape. With rheumatoid arthritis.

You have to accept who you are wholeheartedly, completely and without lying to yourself. If you're a nosy old broad, admit it. It's okay to be a nosy old broad. If you're an anal-retentive young man, don't tell yourself you're precise and detail-oriented. You're anal-retentive. It's okay. Accept and you can understand why you're a nosy old broad and why you're an anal-retentive young man and you can take steps to change if you need to. And if you don't really need to—after all, being nosy may be annoying to your friends but it doesn't actually harm anyone— self-acceptance will at least give you joy in who you are.

### E x e r c i s e

No self-analysis is needed at this stage. Just look in the mirror and accept what you see. So you're overweight. That body also brought three wonderful children into the world. You're impatient. Well, maybe you have a lot to do and the fools insist on getting in your way. Accept, then understand, then change. Not the other way around.

# 72

# Intensity overcomes obstacles

As a martial arts teacher, I have seen (repeatedly) students who don't have a lot of talent achieve more than students who do have a lot of talent. These less talented students have intensity. They have heart. They see the obstacle and they determine to overcome it. The more talented student sees his talent is not equal to the obstacle and gives up.

Intensity might be called focus or heart or passion. It's the grit that makes a person go forward even if she's not confident that the obstacle can be overcome. She just knows she's going to give it her best shot.

I have known martial artists with heart disease and liver problems who have earned black belts, deaf martial artists and physically disabled martial artists who have achieved their martial arts goals. I know of a blind martial arts teacher. Yet at the same time, many people without special problems have abandoned their martial arts goals. These people with disabilities have learned that intensity helps them compensate for their losses, and helps them achieve goals in a way that able-bodied people may never have to learn. The less talented students I have taught may have learned the same lesson, whereas the more talented people may never have had to.

Intensity overcomes obstacles. If you're passionate about achieving your goals, you will.

Feel passionate about something (I said *something*, not *someone*). Enjoy your enthusiasm. Build on it. Maybe you love berry-picking. How can berry-picking overcome obstacles? Maybe it just serves as an excellent diversion from an otherwise boring life. Maybe it's a hobby you can do with your kids (you were looking for that). Or maybe you start a berry-picking operation, thus being able to give up your boring job as a data-entry clerk. More important, you'll learn how to apply that intensity of feeling to other goals and obstacles in your life so that you can achieve your goals and overcome the obstacles. Cultivate your passions, and they'll see you through many tough times.

## 73

# The Way is different for everyone

I am told that there are people in the world who don't actually practice martial arts. I find this hard to believe given how many benefits people get from training in the martial arts. But I know the martial arts are not for everyone. Some people don't find them appealing. Some people simply don't have the time to commit to them. Does this mean they will never find the Way?

Of course not. The Way is different for everyone. Some people can quite contentedly find a life of balance and moderation, attending to mind-body-spirit, without ever learning how to punch people. I may think they're missing out, but as long as they're on the Way, I don't care.

How do you find the Way? In a sense, the Way finds you. If you're unhappy, dissatisfied and bored, you're not on the Way. Maybe you were once on the Way but you have obviously fallen off.

Of course, you can be on the Way and still feel pain and grief and sorrow. At the same time, you also know that you are on the Way. The pain and sorrow has to do with your experiences—your cat died, your mother has cancer—not the way you're living your life. If you have no reason to be dissatisfied, unhappy and bored, and yet you are, you need to open yourself to finding the Way.

You do not necessarily need to go in pursuit of the Way. (In fact, the Way is trying to find you.) Sit still for a minute and let the Way do its job.

Maybe the Way for you requires you to get a certain job. Maybe you need to volunteer at the soup kitchen. Maybe you need to join a Buddhist monastery. I'm practically certain, though, that the Way does not require a big screen TV and a new wardrobe, but I've been wrong before.

Where does your heart lead you? That's the Way trying to talk to you. Sit still and listen.

### Exercise

If you feel you've found the Way (or at least a Way), don't think you're wrong just because other people do it differently. If, however, you're in doubt or you know you haven't found the Way, then you need to spend some quiet time resting and reflecting. What feels discordant about your life? Where is your life in conflict with your heart? You don't need to trek to Tibet to find the

Way but if your heart tells you to go there, then find a way. Maybe the process of getting there will show you the Way. Maybe you'll find that the process of saving money to go to Tibet is what helps you find the Way. Maybe you'll go to graduate school, following your heart, assuming the Way means for you to become a college teacher. But, once you move to the college town, you find a martial arts school, and realize that you're supposed to be a martial artist, not an English teacher. (The Way can be surprising. You're on your way to do one thing when the Way shows you what you should be doing.)

## 74

## Disharmony shatters focus

Two oxen, of equal strength, yoked together, going in the same direction, can do a lot of work. When they start pulling in opposite directions, watch out.

Disharmony shatters focus. Worry, doubt, confusion, fear—all interfere with harmony. If you're trying to write a letter and all you can think about is how late your teenage son is, that will be one tough letter to write.

The fighter knows that fear makes it difficult to defeat the opponent. The fighter must be calm and confident—in harmony—to defeat the opponent. Staying in harmony and finding balance is important not only because it's healthy by its very nature, but also because lack of harmony shatters focus.

A family in constant conflict cannot, individually and collectively, achieve very many goals. A person constantly worrying about money problems or job problems cannot enjoy life's journey. The solution is to create harmony and balance when you can and to dismiss disharmony when you can. You may be able to learn to get along with your husband by getting marital counseling. This will help bring harmony back into your home. If your brother and sister are arguing, and you can't bring harmony to them (sometimes you shouldn't even try), you can leave the room (or the house), remind yourself it isn't your problem, do some deep breathing and regain your inner harmony.

Although it's natural for people to have conflict occasionally, constant conflict isn't healthy. You cannot grow, achieve, enjoy the Way, if you're constantly faced with disharmony.

### Exercise

A great deal of disharmony could be resolved in people's lives if they—and those around them—followed basic rules of courtesy. The rules are simple. Devise a list, explain the rules to your family and enforce them. For instance, a teenager might have a midnight curfew. If he will be late, he must call. Calling mitigates but does not eliminate the punishment for being late. Not calling when he will be late increases the punishment. You may not appreciate his being late, you may not enjoy getting phone calls at three minutes to twelve, and you may be irritated that you have to punish him for being late when it's just as easy for him to be on time, but at least you're not torn between screaming at him and picturing him lying lifeless in the hospital morgue.

If your husband continually leaves all the housework to you, point out the discourtesy of this behavior. Make up a schedule of who does what chores. Get his input. He might hate doing dishes less than he hates doing laundry. Each of you can choose the tasks you don't mind, then split the rest. Leave his tasks undone. If you must do them, pay yourself $75 an hour out of your joint account and buy a new pair of shoes.

Address conflict at work or with friends in a similar direct manner. Avoid unnecessary contact with people who drive you nuts. E-mail and voice mail will do wonders for your sanity. In other words, find strategies for eliminating conflict and disharmony in your life. Work to achieve this goal as you would any goal.

### 75

## Acting with integrity brings freedom

Martial artists are expected to act with integrity. In a simple, basic way, this means that when they train, they give their training their best effort, even when no one is looking. It means they commit to training regularly, even when they don't feel like it. Martial artists understand that they always represent their school and their instructor. If they get into unprovoked fights, they're not representing their school well, and may be asked to leave. A warrior always strives to be as good as her word, not simply because her instructor demands it, but because it is essential to living in harmony with others, and to following the Way. You cannot find the Way if you are dishonest; it requires authenticity and integrity.

Integrity sometimes has a price. If you blow the whistle on your boss, you might lose your job. If you refuse to participate in a fraudulent transaction, you might lose your job. It can get monotonous after a while, and it can be tempting to forget about integrity just this once. But integrity brings freedom.

If you live with integrity, you don't have to worry about the investigator indicting you when the company collapses because you were fired months ago when you refused to participate. You don't have to lie awake at night wondering if you'll lose your coaching job because you don't really have a Master's degree in exercise physiology. You don't have to sneak out to make phone calls to your lover because you won't be cheating on your husband.

Integrity means never having to be ashamed of yourself. And that's a great freedom.

You don't have to worry about keeping your story straight because there is no story to keep straight. You just tell the truth. You don't have to wonder if the skeletons in the closet will ever start rattling around because you won't have any. If you do, but you've lived your life with integrity since, the damage won't be as severe.

The price of integrity is small compared with the price of dishonesty.

Living with integrity means you're not always chiseling for that last dime or misrepresenting the stock offering or taking delight in suckering the sucker. Only a small person would engage in those activities, and you're not a small person. When you live with integrity, you have freedom.

Integrity is more than honesty. It's about being as good as your word. It means when you make a promise, you keep it, so you don't make promises lightly. It means you're the person other people count on. It means your children never have to open the newspaper and find out that you're being investigated for insider trading. Because you have integrity, you live by the rules of society and the rules of your heart.

## Exercise

Integrity starts with small things that no one else will notice. When the cashier undercharges you, you point it out. You're purchasing the products at an agreed-upon price, and just because she saw only three apples in your bag when you had four doesn't mean you get a special four-for-the-price-of-three deal. If the cashier gives you change for a $20 and you gave her a $10, you point it out. Don't rationalize it by saying you've won the cashier lotto, or that the cashier at the drugstore shortchanged you last week and this just evens it up.

At work, do not use the copier for personal business. It costs a nickel per page at the grocery store. You can spring for that. Don't steal office supplies so that you don't have to buy school supplies for your kid. It's not okay and everyone is not doing it. Once you start to make these small statements about your honesty, you'll find it easier to have integrity about bigger things, too. If you're not the kind of person who would steal paper clips, then you're not the kind of person who would steal pension funds, either.

# 76

# Clear mind, correct action

Decisions based on fear, doubt, confusion or anger cannot be relied upon. The warrior knows that if he is fearful or angry when he draws his sword, his opponent has already defeated him.

If you're afraid you're never going to get married, is that a good reason to marry the next man who asks? Isn't it a long-term loving relationship with a man you can raise children with that you're looking for? How would marrying the next man who comes along ensure this? Is being married more important than being married to the right man?

If you don't think you should stay, but you're not sure you should leave, is that the perfect time to strike out on your own? If you and your boyfriend have a big fight, is that the perfect time to dump him, because of course you'll never regret it when you cool off?

Important decisions should be made with a clear mind. Only then can you be assured that you're taking correct action. If, after you've cooled down, you decide that you and your boyfriend really don't have enough in common to stay together, then you can make a correct, rational decision to break up with him.

At the same time, because you've made a calm, rational decision, you're less likely to be swayed by his tearful entreaties to give it one more shot. Because you know you didn't make the decision in the heat of the moment, you know that it's the right one. If you're in the grip of emotion yourself, it might make sense to give the relationship one more shot, but as you are now calm and clear-minded, you recall that the last ten attempts to just give it one more shot have ended in spectacular failure. And you can firmly restate your position, which is, not in this lifetime.

Although it's occasionally fun to burn your bridges and cackle as they turn to ash, in general, waiting to make a decision until you have a clear mind will lead to correct action.

If your boss is a jerk and insults you three times a day, it makes sense to decide, with a clear mind, that it's time for a new job. Once you find a new job, then, and only then, make your decision known instead of responding to an insult one Friday afternoon only to find yourself without a job Monday morning.

### Exercise

To act with a clear mind, recognize when you're feeling angry, upset and fearful. If you're being pressured to do or say something or make a decision, you'll have to deliberately calm down. Tell the other party that you have to take a moment to think about it. (If someone continues to pressure me after I've said this, I tell them the answer is "no," or whatever is the opposite of what they want me to say. They usually back off then and let me think about it.)

Remember, though, that making no decision is also a decision. If you hate your job but never decide to look for a new one, then you are choosing to stay with a job you hate. Instead of falling into that trap, give yourself time to clear your mind. Calm down, collect your wits, take a couple of deep breaths, brew some tea, meditate, do a little yoga. In short, do what is needed to clear your mind. Then you will know the correct action to take, so take it.

## 77

# The universe wants to be in rhythm with you

Martial artists, when they fight, naturally fall into rhythm with each other. This tendency is so common and so pronounced that fighters have to actually practice broken rhythm training in order to break the habit.

Why is rhythm a problem for a fighter? Because it's easier to anticipate what a fighter in rhythm will do, compared with a fighter not in rhythm. Even so, it's more fun to spar when you are in rhythm with each other. It's deeply satisfying, like having a good partner in an unusual dance.

There are other aspects of martial arts that tap into rhythm, such as doing repetitive kicks and performing forms. Each of these requires rhythmic movements.

The theory of synchronization suggests that the universe wants to be in rhythm. That's why women who live together have menstrual cycles that (unless artificially regulated) eventually synchronize with each other. Your heart beats in a rhythm. For it to beat in arrhythmia usually means a serious cardiac disorder. Our longing for rhythm is why we find non-rhythmic patterns and sounds so irritating.

We are meant to be in rhythm with the universe and

the universe wants to be in rhythm with us. This does not mean you have to go live in the country and get in touch with nature and learn to appreciate the joys of bunny rabbits. It does mean that you should be aware of your connection to the world, to the people milling around you on a city sidewalk, to the special feel of spring sunshine, to the delight of the wind in your face during a scorcher of a day. (Unless, of course, the wind is a windstorm, in which case taking cover would be the more prudent course of action.)

It means appreciating your hound dog as a creature of the universe who has just as much right to exist as you do, and taking a few moments to just be with him, enjoying the doggy breath and the equally delightful doggy kisses, and not muttering about how you don't have time for this.

### Exercise

One of the reasons we find schedules so comforting is the sense of rhythm (and, of course, control) they impose on our lives. But overscheduling creates frustration and burnout because our lives have a natural rhythm, too. Some days it's just healthy to laze in bed and sleep until noon.

Finding your natural rhythm is healthy. If you're a morning person, adjust your schedule to accommodate for that. If you're a night person, you can do the same. If obligations prevent you, you can at least ease the problem by remaining consistent and learning to appreciate the joys of the schedule you do have. If you're a night person but must work a day job, you can learn to appreciate the coolness of the morning and the sense of accomplishment you feel when you've finished six tasks before eight A.M.

# 78

# Don't show your power to anyone

The *Tae Te Ching,* which is not exactly a warrior's manual, nonetheless chimes in now and then on what a warrior should do. Or not do, as the case may be.

Don't show your power to anyone, the *Tae Te Ching* warns.

If you show your opponent what you can do, your opponent can devise a strategy for defeating you. If he knows you're a Karate master, he might avoid Karate weapons. If he doesn't know, he won't be able to formulate an effective strategy—or, at least, not so effective a strategy.

If you constantly crow about your prowess in Karate, sooner or later someone is going to come along, listen to you and punch you in the nose. Then you're going to look and feel pretty stupid. Claiming expert status, talking about how tough you are, only challenges people to try you. Why waste time and energy battling people who would not bother you if you weren't so convinced of your superiority to all other Karate masters? Sure, you might win all the battles, but you're wasting a lot of time and energy, and what's the point? A warrior knows that you fight only when you have to and when you have a reasonable objective to attain. (Proving how tough you are does not meet this criteria.)

Let people discover for themselves that you can bend iron bars into knots. Don't take an ad out in the newspaper or you'll have swarms of people knocking on your door with iron bars. (You may think this is good marketing strategy, but an even better one is to let word of mouth do your work for you.)

Keep your power to yourself and you won't have to constantly spend it. This principle can apply to other points as well. For the most part, you can and should keep your business and personal dealings to yourself; at the minimum, you should keep them in their separate spheres. Talking about your ex-husband at work can make you seem unbusinesslike and can undermine your credibility; talking about your work to your friends, especially if you talk too much, makes you a boring person.

Even more important, keeping your mouth shut prevents people from having leverage over you. If you constantly talk about your work taking you away from your kids, and a job promotion opens up, your boss may simply not consider you for the position because you already have work-home conflicts and she doesn't think you can handle more. Maybe that's fine, maybe you don't want the promotion, maybe it would take you away from the kids more and you'd rather not. But that should be your decision to make. If you've been angling for that promotion for years, you've just sabotaged yourself. Either way, wanting the promotion or not, refraining from talking too much about your personal life at work would have meant you would be given the choice to pursue the promotion.

You can prevent problems in your personal life by not dwelling on your work life to the exclusion of all else. Certainly friends and family want to know how things are going but the general outlines are sufficient. "We're starting a new project, so lots of meetings right now," is probably as much as your next-door neighbor needs to know.

There are several reasons for this. First, you never know who your opponent is. Okay, so it's probably not your aged grandmother. But we have all had friends who worked for businesses in direct competition with us, or else they had friends or spouses who did. An innocent remark could unwittingly give away important information to a competitor. Second, the people in your life want you to focus on them when you're with them, not on your work. They might rightfully think you find your work more important than they are if that's all you can talk about. Third, talking about ideas, plans and projects before they're ready can dissipate your energy, creativity and passion for them. Sure, brainstorming can help you solve a problem or come up with an idea, but we've all had the experience where we talked so much about something we were going to do that when the time came to do it, we really didn't feel like doing it after all. A good example of this is the book you're going to write someday. If you tell everyone you meet all the plot details and who you based the characters on, you may never get around to writing the book. Your impetus—wanting to share this great story—will be gone, because you've already shared it with everyone you've met for the past ten years.

## Exercise

If you're in the habit of sharing more information than you need to, make a specific, conscious effort to think about what you're saying before you say it. Be especially careful to keep work and personal lives separate. If you already have work friendships based on sharing personal lives, you don't need to abandon them, but you have to be careful. It would be prudent for you to monitor what you say and to be careful about revealing too much about your personal life. Keep topics safe and neutral whenever possible. Talk about Timmy's soccer game, and not how he got into the liquor cabinet last Friday. If you think friendship can't grow this way, you're right. But friendships with people you meet at work are tricky. They usually aren't true friendships anyway (most don't survive when either friend leaves the company). They should not be considered more than they are. You would be better off developing friendships outside of the work environment.

## 79
# Sometimes you yield, sometimes you stand your ground

An Aikidoist knows that if you yield, you can defeat an attacker. If he strikes, you shift away and the attack is harmless. Sometimes you counter with a joint lock to disable the attacker.

A principle of self-defense is that not everything is worth fighting over. Even the most experienced fighter knows that the outcome of any street fight can never be determined in advance. You don't know if your attacker has a knife or a gun or a buddy around the corner. You don't know if your attacker is trained in boxing or the martial arts. You don't know if he's drunk or high. You might be able to make a fairly accurate guess, but any of these factors can make your winning the fight more difficult.

Responsible self-defense instructors will teach you

that the first and best thing to do when confronted by a potential attack is to walk away, if you can do so safely. So what if the guy standing on the corner has just called you a very unkind name? That reflects badly on him, not on you. No need to take offense and go punch him out. Just walk away. Even if (gasp!) he calls you a coward.

If someone grabs your purse or demands your wallet, give it to him (yield). No need to end up in the emergency room getting fifty-seven stitches in your face because you decided to hang on to your wallet. It's not worth it.

It should go without saying that while you're being mugged, you should get a good look at the mugger (no, no, not so you'll remember him next time you meet and you'll be prepared, but so you can call the cops, report the crime and identify the miscreant). Remember, hair color and cut can be changed, beards and mustaches can be grown and shaved. Focus on the size of the attacker, compared to you, the apparent ethnicity, including hints like a Southern drawl, any distinctive characteristics like scars and tattoos. The color of the eyes and the shape of the face can also be remembered.

You can't manage this if you're in a terrified panic, so remember that a calm mind leads to correct action.

Just as there are times when you yield, there are times when you stand your ground. While only you can decide which is which, when you're physically attacked (or when someone you love is attacked), then you do what you have to do.

## Exercise

Our pet peeves waste a lot of time and energy. Fighting against things we cannot change drains energy. We don't have the time or passion left over to fight the important battles. If your husband is ten minutes late to everything, accept that he is ten minutes late to everything, and stop feeling angry and frustrated about it. If he hasn't changed by now, he is never going to change.

On the other hand, stand your ground when you need to. If your boss tells off-color jokes at work, that's not okay. It doesn't mean you're not a team player or you have no sense of humor if you object. It means the boss telling off-color jokes at work is inappropriate and he needs to stop.

## 80

## Train outside the *dojo*

The new martial artist is frequently very excited about what she is learning and tries to absorb as much information as possible. She watches every Bruce Lee movie ever made, picks up magazines with titles like *Legends of the Karate Masters* (that she would have scornfully bypassed only weeks before). After some time, her initial enthusiasm settles into a quieter kind of dedication that she can sustain for years to come.

Sometimes, though, the martial artist thinks that training can only take place in the *dojo*. She divorces what she learns in the *dojo* from her "real" life. If she thinks of her training outside the *dojo*, she puts it in the context of, "I'll know what to do if I'm attacked by a crazed mugger."

But you should train outside the *dojo*. Literally, yes. You should actually practice your techniques in different places to get a practical understanding of how they work. If you're wearing workboots or sandals or four-inch heels, your ability to do certain kicks will be altered. You may not want to do jump spinning wheel kicks in heels. You may not be able to pivot very easily in heavy workboots. You learn to modify the techniques. Maybe instead of pivoting in those boots, you step into the kick.

Performing a technique on a flat indoor surface is different from doing them in the backyard or in a parking lot. What you can do in your Judo uniform may not be so effective when you're wearing tight-fitting jeans and the other guy is shirtless.

By training outside the *dojo*, you'll also be open to learning new techniques. If your style teaches only kicks and punches, you can attend a seminar on grappling and learn some basics in case you're ever confronted with the situation where someone throws you to the ground.

Training outside the *dojo* reminds you that you're always a warrior. If you're training to master the techniques of Karate, you don't leave the *dojo*, go home, light up a cigarette and knock off six beers. That defeats the training.

You also apply what you've learned to your life outside the *dojo*. That's what this book is about. If you learn that perseverance helps you succeed inside the *dojo*, then you should be able to apply that lesson to your life outside the *dojo*.

## Exercise

Think of yourself as an athlete "in training" even if you're not a martial artist. If you're trying to lose weight and a friend offers you a doughnut, you can refuse it politely by saying, "I'm in training." It doesn't matter if your friend thinks you're joking. You can park your car a couple of blocks from work and walk the rest of the way in because you're in training. You can choose healthier food because you're in training. "Training" should be something that affects all aspects of your life, and isn't just for pro athletes.

81

## Don't resist your potential

To reach your potential takes a lot of work. To learn to do the jump spinning wheel kick takes more effort than not learning it does. A martial artist realizes that her body can do things she never believed possible. At the same time, she realizes that learning these things will take time and effort and maybe a couple of bruises.

It's easy to resist your potential. You could try out for the high school football team, but you're too little for anyone to give you a scholarship to college, so why bother?

It's comfortable to stay with what's safe. If you've always yearned to be a painter but know how to be an accountant, it can be hard to give up the safety of numbers to become an artist.

We all have more potential than we ever fulfill. We can do more with our bodies than we do; we can do more with our minds and with our hearts. But time after time, we resist our potential.

There are facile explanations. We fear failure. If we try out for the play the community theater is putting on, and we don't get the part, then maybe that will show us we're not as talented as we think we are. If we don't go to the tryouts, we can tell ourselves, "I could get that part if I did try."

We fear success. If we do graduate from college, then maybe our relationship with our family will change. Maybe we'll have to get a more challenging job.

The truth is, we resist our potential because fulfilling it would require change. It would mean watching less television and eating more green vegetables. It would mean trying new things you might not like when you like the old things perfectly well. Change is loss. No one wants to lose things. Even overcoming an addiction is a loss. Without those cigarettes or that bottle of Scotch in hand, now how are you going to get through the day?

To grow, however, you have to embrace your potential. You have to be willing to change and to lose. Imagine what you could be if you were able to accept the number of possibilities open to you—if only you were willing to do the work.

We all have practically unlimited potential. We don't all have potential for exactly the same things. You may have the potential to be a brilliant singer, whereas your friend has the potential to be a great dancer. But we all have potential to be better people, more honest, more loving to our children, more patient with the garrulous old folks next door. Don't fear the losses. The Way requires you to lose in order to gain.

### Exercise

Have you lived up to your potential in all areas of your life? Where do you feel you have particularly failed to fulfill your promise? What has stopped you? What changes and losses would fulfilling your potential require? Do you know these changes or losses would occur or do you just think they might and use them as an excuse for not doing the work? Try to start associating more with people you admire, who you think have fulfilled or are fulfilling their potential. Ask about their "secrets." You may find the things they feared never happened, or that they did happen, but were overcome with work and effort.

82

## Pace yourself in training and you'll never exceed your limits

"Pace yourself" is a cry we hear frequently (usually when we're about to beat everyone in the pack). "Pace yourself" has meaning if you're running a marathon. Start too strong and you'll run out of energy before you hit the finish line.

But much of life is a sprint. A martial arts class, which might last an hour, is a sprint. If you don't push yourself, you'll never increase your endurance or build your muscle mass.

Pace yourself in training and you'll pace yourself in life. Pace yourself in training and you'll never exceed your limits.

The reason a weight lifter lifts a weight repeatedly until her muscle fails—she can't lift anymore—is to build a stronger muscle. When the muscle fails, the body says, "Uh-oh. We need to get stronger," then tears down the muscle and builds a stronger one in its place. With this stronger muscle in place, the weight lifter doesn't just stop lifting weights. Now she has to increase the amount of weight she lifts until the muscle fails again, so it can grow stronger. This process goes on for a very long time, and even once a weight lifter reaches her absolute maximum capacity, she continues to push her muscles to failure in order to stay strong.

A martial artist pushes herself in training to the point where she is exhausted at the end of training. She has given it her all. What would be the point of saving it? By giving the training session every ounce of her energy, she grows stronger and develops more endurance and can do even more next time.

By consistently pushing yourself to give more and do better, you'll exceed your limits. It's also incredibly satisfying to come to the end of a class—or a day—where you've given it your all. You know you gave it your best. It feels good. Too often we give it only what is necessary to get by. But by pushing it, we'll discover strengths we didn't know we had. We'll learn to dig deep and find more strength—emotional or physical, mental or spiritual. But that strength won't be there when we need it if we pace ourselves.

Give each day and each effort your best shot. (If it's not worth your best shot, why are you doing it?) Practice being in the moment. Pay attention to the article you're reading, thoroughly proofread that e-mail before you send it out. Be completely satisfied with the proposal before submitting it to the client. Push yourself to move beyond competent to good and beyond good to great.

## 83

# Breakthroughs happen as the result of sustained effort

Persistence and perseverance are essential to success in any area of life. Too often, though, we give up too soon or sell ourselves short, believing we could never achieve a goal that is important to us. Often, we do give a goal a repeated effort, yet we find we do not achieve it. The problem is that perseverance without the ability to evaluate and criticize your performance is fruitless and disheartening. Perseverance means never letting rejection or failure keep you from attaining your goal, but it also requires evaluating the means you use to reach your goal.

In martial arts, we most often talk about perseverance in relation to physical performance. A person may wish to kick head-high. He or she may even practice it repeatedly.

But without muscle strength and flexibility, the goal will never be reached. A larger goal can be achieved only by defining and mastering the smaller goals necessary to acquire it.

In some cases, we have all the information we need about our performance, and we have achieved the smaller goals necessary to master it, and we still cannot reach the goal. In that case, continued effort is required for long periods of time. Having enough heart to do this is the sign of a true warrior. A kick must be repeated 10,000 times before you know how to do it. Having the heart to do that kick 10,000 times is warrior spirit.

Sustained effort is required to achieve breakthroughs. Martial artists sometimes reach plateaus where they don't feel they're making progress. Only by continued effort does the breakthrough occur, sometimes dramatically. All of a sudden, you can do that kick. All of a sudden, you can defeat that black belt in point sparring.

## Exercise

Identify one area of your life where you struggle and give up. Perhaps it's your tennis game. Perhaps you can never get along with your boss and always quit your job. Maybe every time you start a needlework project, you never finish it. Commit to solving the problem or succeeding at your goal. But create a plan for reaching it, and devise a way to evaluate your progress. If you need to master other skills first, learn them. If you need to change your approach, change it. Maybe you need to hire a different coach for your tennis. Perhaps you should go back to school so that you can get jobs that have more interesting challenges. Or maybe you should become your own boss. Maybe you need to try quilting instead of needlepoint. Regardless, make a firm commitment to yourself that you will never give up this goal no matter what. It must be a heartfelt commitment, not, "I'll try to do better at tennis next week." Instead, commit to a statement like, "I'm going to work on my serve for twenty minutes a day, three days a week, and get in at least one game a week with a better opponent." Then do it.

## 84

### Embrace the dragon

According to martial arts legend, Shaolin temple monks who were ready to become masters would strip naked and embrace a fiery hot vessel carved with the pictures of a dragon and a tiger (two favorite martial arts emblems). The experience would leave scars on the monks' bodies (and probably on their psyches, too). The scar on their bodies resembled a dragon and a tiger. The test would prove their courage and ability to overcome their fears. Who really wants to undergo a procedure that's going to hurt a lot and leave scars?

Although you probably won't ever have to embrace a red-hot vessel with a dragon embossed on it, there will be times in your life when you're faced with a dragon, figuratively speaking, and you'll have to do something about it.

What you have to do is embrace the dragon.

The dragon is pain. It is fear or anger, or whatever keeps you from happiness, from success, from mastery. Through the dragon, you will learn wisdom, but it will hurt. The dragon has been around for millennia, and will be around for all eternity. It knows a great deal. It can teach you much. But not if you're constantly trying to slay the dragon. Not if you try to pretend that dragons don't exist.

When my daughter was born with a serious genetic disorder, I spent a couple of months waiting for someone to tell me that they had been mistaken and that my daughter didn't have this dreadful disease after all. Instead, she began to have intractable seizures that no medication could control. She had extensive brain surgery when she was nine months old to help stop the seizures.

That was when I finally embraced the dragon. I finally accepted that my daughter was dreadfully ill, and that there was no cure. There might be treatments, but no cure. I accepted that she was cognitively impaired and had numerous medical problems and physical disabilities.

But the dragon made me see how strong she was (and how strong I was). The dragon made me see how brave she was, and how tenacious and stubborn. I didn't need to compare her to other children her age. She would surely come up short. But she had things they lacked. She had character already! When she wasn't even one year old!

The dragon taught me patience and acceptance. The dragon taught me to live the life I was given. The dragon taught me to disregard other people's expectations and demands. So what if I don't live in a house in the suburbs? I never wanted one. That was someone else's dream.

As she grew older and could do more, physically and cognitively, and I had gotten to spend time with her and find out what kind of a character she really was, I was still afraid that she would die of the disease. After I'd had her for that long, there was no way I could lose her and still say sane.

So I embraced *that* dragon. I acknowledged that I was afraid she would die. I admitted that she could die and leave me all alone in the world. I cried about it for two days. I couldn't imagine what life would be like without her. I would have to kill myself. (I get a bit theatrical when I'm in pain.) But the dragon taught me that even if she died, we could have a wonderful life together for all the days she had to give.

Which is not to say that she doesn't exasperate me on a regular basis. But I know I am now more loving toward her and more patient than I would be otherwise. I make time for her even though work awaits. The work will always be there. I accept that she might leave long before I am ready, but I will face that dragon when it arrives. I don't hold her at arm's length because I'm afraid. She snuggles right next to my heart.

### Exercise

We often try to protect ourselves by staying uncommitted or by keeping our arms crossed and our hearts closed. If you adopt a cat and love it, someday it will die. If you start a family tradition, someday it will end. Too often, we think, why bother? It will only cause pain. But the dragon teaches us what it means to be human, and that's a lesson worth learning. Embrace the dragon. Accept that life has losses. If there were no losses, we could never know moments of pure, transcendent joy.

So go adopt that cat. Enjoy every moment you have. Accept that it's not forever. Life is beautiful anyway. Maybe because of that.

## 85

# Someone else's win is not always your loss

Fighters tend to view competition in a straightforward way. They compete; they either win or they lose. If the other guy has won, generally that means you have lost. But not always. The martial artist know that when she trains, she will not always be able to defeat her partner/opponent. She knows that fighting superior fighters makes her a better fighter. So if she loses a match but has improved her fighting skills, she hasn't "lost" anything. But if all she does is keep score, she will never become a better fighter. If all she will fight are fighters who are less skilled than she is, she will never become a better fighter.

We're often jealous of other people's wins. If a friend gets a new promotion or a new car or an inheritance, it's hard not to feel, "Why can't that be me?" Often we think of all the reasons the other person doesn't deserve the win. They don't work that hard, they're not generous to others, they break the rules.

An adult, however, should be able to set aside these feelings and be happy for his or her friends. If your competitive instinct is aroused, ask yourself if you're just being ridiculous and jealous, or if you really should be doing more with your life. A few years ago, I read about a writer who had published seven books by the time he had reached my age. I thought I had been doing really well with three. But that spark of jealousy made me think that maybe I could work harder on my writing (and I could). When I was finally satisfied with my level of work and my output, it never bothered me to read about someone who had written more than I had. I knew I was doing the best I could while still maintaining a balance in my life.

On the other hand, when a friend won a writing grant, and I felt jealous, it was ridiculous of me to do so. I don't need writing grants; I'm not interested in applying for them. It's just that someone had what I didn't, and wasn't it childish of me to want it for my own? Of course. I was able to recognize this right away and be sincerely happy for my friend.

When we feel we lack in comparison to others, we need to do something about it. We can quit comparing ourselves to others. (There will always be people who write more books than I do, or who get paid more money for them, or who sell more copies. And there will always be people who write fewer books than I do, get paid less and sell fewer copies.) We can do something about it (other than feel jealous). Or we can firmly dismiss our jealousy as an unproductive emotion.

We should remind ourselves that we don't all share the same values and have the same gifts. Be happy for your brother when he can afford the forty-six-foot cruiser even though you're barely scraping by driving a secondhand Yugo. You chose your life, and there are very good reasons you live in that apartment and drive that car. (Write the reasons down if you have to.) Besides, if you're genuinely happy for your brother, he'll probably let you go cruising in the boat as much as you want.

Remember, someone else's win is not always your loss.

The next time someone wins and you want to know why it isn't you, ask yourself if you've really lost. Do you really want to own a six-bedroom mansion on the golf course? Who would scrub all those toilets? Are you really that pretentious? Would it mean you have to scrimp over everything else? Or stay up all night wondering how the hell you're going to pay for it? Lots of people own things they can't afford and keep taking second mortgages out on their homes to afford them. Is that how you want to live, just so you can impress the poor relations?

If the truth is you do look bad by comparison, you can still be happy for your friend while at the same time vowing to do better. If your friend just graduated from college, which has always been a dream of yours, be happy for her, then enroll in night school. If it wouldn't be too hard on your pride, ask her how she did it. She might have plenty of helpful advice for you.

## 86

# If you act with integrity, everything you do will be powerful

The martial artist knows that confidence and determination help create personal power. A fighter who is hesitant or doubtful will deliver feeble blows, while the confident, determined fighter will commit to powerful strikes.

In martial arts, this confidence and determination stems from the knowledge that you know what you are doing, and you know that you are doing it correctly. In martial arts, commitment to training and a certain amount of experience will give you this confidence.

In our daily lives, our personal power comes from living with integrity. When we live with integrity, we know what we are doing and we know that we are doing it correctly.

This doesn't mean we can or will turn into smug, self-righteous prigs (being self-righteous violates the principle of integrity). It means we will have the calm confidence that we're making the right decisions, even if the right decision has bad consequences. For example, you blow the whistle on your company's illegal dumping practices. You promptly get fired. You know that you have done what is right and just. I realize that being right and just doesn't pay the bills, but countenancing illegal, unethical and immoral activities—sanctioning them by not saying anything about them or doing anything to stop them—makes us equally culpable. We're guilty of being an accessory to a crime when we don't do anything about it. The emotional, mental or spiritual costs of this complicity are enormous. We often forget about this harm that we're doing to ourselves when we're worried about our jobs. We think the job loss would be more serious than the loss of self-respect. We would be wrong. You can always get another job. It's hard to live with yourself once you've destroyed your self-respect.

By choosing to live with integrity, you'll be confident and powerful. (As certain friends say about me, I am occasionally wrong but never in doubt.) Knowing what you should do is very powerful. Not everyone has this skill. Most people don't want to know what they should do because it might require some painful sacrifices. But living with integrity gives you control. You're not just waiting for events to spin out of control. You take charge. All actions that come from conviction are powerful.

When people know that you are a person of integrity, they trust you. They know what you say is true. They know if you promise it, you will do it. There are few people in the world who are reliable, and others looks up to them as leaders.

The world is full of petty people who cheat on their taxes and pad their expense accounts. Don't sell yourself that cheaply. If you're going to lose your integrity and self-respect, it shouldn't be for a two-bit job or a promotion in a two-bit company. Sadly, we lose our integrity and self-respect for stakes so small it should make you weep.

Set your price high. Your integrity is what makes you powerful, and if you give it away, you become weak. Living with integrity in all things may make you unpopular some-times, but you will have the power of confidence and self-respect. And a clear conscience.

### Exercise

Your word should be meaningful. As hard as it is to say "no" to people, it is necessary to living with integrity. If Geraldine in accounting invites you over for Sunday brunch so you can see her doll collection, and you say "yes" so as not to hurt her feelings but have every intention of coming down with a splitting headache on Sunday morning, you are not living with integrity.

Practice integrity in small things first. Notice how good it feels to stop lying. (It goes without saying that you won't need-lessly hurt people's feelings. "No, thank you," is what you say to

Geraldine, not, "No, thanks, I think grown adults with doll collections are imbecilic and pitiable and I couldn't be bothered to waste my time like that.")

Once you regain control of your personal integrity in small things, you can begin to use it in larger things so that when your boss says, "Shred those files," and your personal alarm bells go off, you can say, "No," even understanding that this is going to cost you. But it would be worse if you say "yes."

## 87

# The Path is sometimes straight and sometimes circular

Just as the warrior learns direct strikes and circular defenses, just as he learns that he should sometimes yield and sometimes stand his ground, so, too, does he learn that the Path is sometimes straight and sometimes circular.

A journey toward any significant goal is never without obstacles. Sometimes you have to take the long way around the obstacle. This can be annoying, but it can also show you secrets about the obstacle that you couldn't have learned by staring at it, trying to go through it or trying to climb over it.

When you embark on a fitness journey, for instance, you may find the first few weeks or months are easy. You eat right, work out, lose weight, gain muscle. You say, "What's so hard about this?" and *blam!* Here comes a wall. An obstacle. Something interferes with your progress. You plateau. You quit gaining strength. You quit losing weight. In fact, you gained three pounds last week, and you couldn't lift as much weight as you did the week before.

You can try to bull straight through, doing everything exactly the same. Or you can drop the whole thing entirely and go back to being a Cheeto-eating sloth. You can try to get over the obstacle by working out even more and eating even less.

Or you can sit down, look at the obstacle and figure out a way around it. Maybe you need to back off a little— you're overtraining. Maybe you're not getting enough protein in your diet to fuel that muscle growth. Maybe it's time to do a different kind of cardio. Maybe you should drop an aerobics class and take a yoga class. Maybe you need a vacation. Maybe you need an adventure.

By going around the obstacle, taking the circular path, you'll learn about the obstacle—what causes it, how to navigate it. The next time you hit a plateau, you can use the strategies you learned previously to get around it.

Meanwhile, you'll enjoy the journey more. You might find that you like yoga much more than aerobics class, so much so that you learn to meditate, go to workshops or seminars and feel refreshed and inspired by your experiences.

But the Way isn't about meeting your goals—it isn't about goals at all. The Way is about becoming a better, more enlightened person. The Way isn't concerned with the outward aspect of your life. It is concerned with the inner aspect. Sometimes, when we're on the Way, the Path is straight. We know where we're going, we feel good about it. It's easy to stay on the Path when it's straight.

But the Way is sometimes circular. You may have

started out driving to Nebraska but ended up in Arizona because you can't read a map, but in Arizona you found a guru who could teach you. You may have intended to retire to Key West but found yourself in a remote Alaskan village where they desperately needed a doctor.

The Path is sometimes straight and sometimes circular. But it still leads where you want to go.

### Exercise

The Path isn't always easy to follow. But it is always worthwhile. Remember, the Path is different for everyone, so no one can tell you how you should follow the Way. However, if you feel unfulfilled, restless, frustrated and unhappy with your life, and this is not owing to a specific problem you're trying to solve (such as a job you hate and are trying to replace), and if you have felt this way for more than a week or two (moods come and go), you may need to recommit yourself to the Path. If you feel that you face challenges but that you're growing and "getting there," you've just hit a circular patch and should just be patient. The Path will become straight again sooner or later (and for at least a little while).

## 88

# The nature of the scorpion is to sting

There's an old martial arts story that goes . . . never mind. It's a long story and in the end, the scorpion stings the hippo that so nicely agreed to bring it across the river, drowning everyone, thus proving the moral of the story, which is, the nature of the scorpion is to sting. The point of the story is to warn the naive and gullible from being taken advantage of by someone they know they should not trust, but who claims to have changed.

In martial arts, this story is used as a way of communicating self-defense principles. A basic premise of self-defense is that we are often victimized by people we know, and we can defend ourselves from these "attacks" simply by being cautious about who we allow into our lives. Self-defense starts with taking care in our relationships with others. In other words, watch out for scorpions.

In the world outside the *dojo*, we want to believe that people can change. We want to believe that people can regret past actions, reform and become better. And they can. Just don't count on it. If a person has abused your trust in the past, it's unwise to let her abuse you again, even if you think trusting her will "help" her become trustworthy. This is a fallacy. People are trustworthy or they're not; you cannot "help" someone who is not trustworthy become trustworthy by trusting him. You merely prove to him, again, how easy it is to fool trustworthy people.

The idea that people can change is a given in our society, and it reflects well on us. But we also believe a harmful correlation, which is that we can change other people. We can't. We can change ourselves. That's it. We don't have magic powers. But we believe we do. The idea that we can help others change is what keeps abused women with their abusive partners (or one of the reasons). It keeps us in unhealthy relationships we know we should get out of. It keeps us from making needed changes in our lives.

The truth is, to truly change requires work. No one

wants to hear this. They think a person can go to sleep a hardened criminal, have a change of heart and wake up a kind, caring individual who only wants to solve the world's problems. Of course, it's in the hardened criminal's best interest for us to believe this fairy tale. The impulse to change, the moment of enlightenment, may strike us in the middle of the night, but the change itself requires real work. If the person who claims to have changed really has, you should see some sign of it. The alcoholic would stay out of bars, would start attending AA meetings and would stop associating with his drinking buddies. Absent these changes, the alcoholic is not recovering; he is still an alcoholic, albeit one with good intentions.

### Exercise

It's human nature to take people at face value. We would rather trust people than not trust them (being suspicious of the motives of others is exhausting work). But, of course, trusting where it is unwarranted can be dangerous.

Develop a sense of caution. Withhold judgment about people until you've gotten to know them. In our electronic world, we create a false sense of intimacy by chatting with people in chat rooms, via bulletin boards and through e-mail. But we have no idea who is really on the other end. In our "real" world encounters, we at least have reliable references—our friends know a person who becomes our friend, our co-worker introduces us to a family member who becomes a friend. These references don't guarantee the person's general trustworthiness, but at least when Cousin Lisa says you should meet her friend Joe the Banker, you can be pretty sure Joe is a banker and not a twelve-year-old boy with a computer in his bedroom.

While it may seem cynical to warn you to be cautious about people's claims, you should remember that people are supposed to *earn* your trust. You don't just give it away. The earning should come in increments. Just because Cousin Lisa vouches for Joe the Banker doesn't mean you should trust him with the keys to your house, the keys to your Corvette and a signed power-of-attorney authorization.

Instead, Joe should prove trustworthy over time. Does he treat you well? Show up when he says he will or call ahead to explain the reason why? Is he nice to your cat and your aged mother? When you let him borrow your car, does he return it with a full tank of gas?

The same strategy is necessary for people who say they've changed. You don't invite the alcoholic ex-wife back into your home and your bank account just on her say so. You start with a few short meetings and you observe. You don't decide ahead of time that she has already changed, thank God, now you can live happily ever after. Prudence will keep you from feeling the scorpion's sting.

## 89

# Frequent encounters with fear make you strong

All fighters face fear. Each time they climb into the ring, their palms are sweaty and their stomachs are queasy. There's nothing in the black-belt manual that teaches you how to be free of fear. (There isn't even a black-belt manual.) The one thing fighters know, though, is that frequent encounters with fear make you strong. They get into the ring not because they enjoy getting punched in the nose, and not necessarily because they enjoy winning (you can win at chess without having any bruises to show for it). They go into the ring because they want to emerge stronger.

When you feel nervous and fearful, and you perform despite your fear, you learn something about yourself. You learn that you are brave. You also learn that you can perform despite your fear.

Suppose you're a martial artist, and you enter a tournament, and you're going to perform your newest form for six judges, who are all seated at a table staring at you. You feel nervous. You think you'll make an idiot of yourself. Well, maybe you will. But you'll survive it, and next time, you'll do better. But most of all, you'll have survived the fearful experience and it won't be half as bad as you might have imagined.

Suppose you enter the sparring competition. Again, you feel nervous and fearful. Your stomach is tied in knots and your muscles feel like water. You know you're never going to be able to hit your opponent. Okay. Maybe you don't. Maybe you lose 16 to 0 and the judges stop the match partway through because you're so inept and you're getting beaten so badly. There will be a next time. Besides, it's better to freeze up in the ring at a tournament than against a crazed attacker, so these competitions you put yourself through are preparing you to meet that attacker. After you've competed a couple of times and worked through your fear, you'll have strategies for handling it. Then if you do meet that crazed attacker, you'll know what to do. Your body will think, "Hell, we've been scared before, no big deal. Let's start with a side kick."

Even if you don't compete in tournaments, you'll be tested on your martial arts knowledge as you make your way up the ranks. Someone—maybe a person you've never met before—will watch you demonstrate your knowledge. That'll leave a lump in your stomach. Performing even though you're scared makes you stronger. At each successive level, you'll do better and you'll learn strategies for overcoming your fear.

Most of us have things that make us fearful. Public speaking, for example, is an activity that terrifies many people. Yet it is often vital to our success to be able to speak to groups.

Other people are afraid of other things. Personally, I'm afraid of those silver, translucent spiders with black markings and extremely pointy legs that grow to be about the size of dinner plates. There are plenty of them where I live now. When I first encountered one as an adult, I shrieked and ran into the bedroom. Repeated encounters have made me stronger, though. I still find them startling and distasteful. They have a habit of materializing in the middle of the room when you least expect it. But when I see one now I just calmly grab the unabridged dictionary and drop it on 'em.

But too often we run shrieking from the room when we're confronted with something we fear. That's not a useful response. Instead, by facing our fears, even exposing ourselves to what we fear, we become stronger. We learn to have power over the fear instead of letting it have power over us.

# Exercise

Face a fear that's holding you back. It might be public speaking, it might be fear of flying. Get help if you need to (and I don't just mean seeing a therapist for fear of flying. Toastmasters, an organization with chapters all over the country, is designed to help its members grow more comfortable with public speaking in a safe environment).

Start in small, safe increments. The second time I encountered one of those unspeakable spiders, I jumped up on a chair. Although it may not seem so, this was an improvement over running shrieking through the house. From this vantage point, I dropped a variety of objects on the spider until it retreated back into the wall from whence it came. The next time, I was prepared. Giving the spider a wide berth, I went into the kitchen where I kept the bug spray. I fumigated the spider until I practically passed out. The spider shrugged and went back into the wall. During the next encounter, I perfected my current technique. Skirting the spider carefully, so as not to alert it to my movements, I went into my office, and got the *Webster's*. I dropped it on the spider. I then jumped up and down on the book a couple of times just to be sure, and then cleaned up the mess. Now I know exactly what to do. By taking small steps but frequently encountering your fear, you will grow stronger, too.

## 90

# A thousand risks are not too many

Most of us live our lives in fear. We take risks, but the risks we take are meaningless or, worse, harmful and dangerous. We smoke when we know it'll cause lung cancer. We drink and drive although we know this is a deadly combination. We drive without wearing our seatbelts even though taking two more seconds to buckle up could save our lives. We even risk our children by not having them in car seats until they're old enough and big enough to wear a regular seatbelt. We eat high-fat diets knowing they cause heart disease. We don't exercise even though we know sedentary lifestyles contribute to obesity and stroke.

In short, we take all the wrong risks, yet are terrified of the ones we should be taking.

By this I mean, we should risk standing up for ourselves at work when the boss takes credit for our great idea again. Instead of staying in the same hateful, boring job—because who else is going to pay us good money to do what we're doing?—we should find more congenial work. We should risk starting that business we've always dreamed of, or writing that book we've always wanted to (and sending it off to publishers). We should try out for the play the community theater is putting on. Or go back to school or get married or get divorced. We need to take risks if we're going to feel satisfied with life.

The fighter knows this. He realizes that any move, any

kick or punch or throw, could be countered or blocked. But he can't win just standing there. He has to risk it.

## Exercise

We fear risk-taking because we don't understand it. We equate risk-taking with "risky" behavior like having unprotected sex. The two could not be further apart. Taking a risk helps you along the path of personal growth. Pursuing risky behavior is just a matter of immediately gratifying yourself (really, how long does it take to put a condom on?). In this case, the focus is on pleasure, not on what could be long-term gains.

Count the number of times you shy away from risk in a given week. Count the number of times you take the chance. The numbers should at least be equal (unless the number is zero, in which case your life needs some serious shaking up). Remember, a thousand risks are not too many.

Consider what is involved in the risk. Does it require time, money, effort? What can you afford to lose? How likely is it that the risk will pan out? What will the reward be if the risk does pan out? It should go without saying that the more you have to lose, the more cautious you should be. But you don't necessarily have to risk a lot at one time in order to gain a lot. When I started martial arts lessons, I paid $60 up front for a few weeks' worth of lessons and $30 for a uniform. Worst case, the whole experience was a disaster. I'd be out $90 and a couple of hours of my time spread over three or four weeks. I could live with that. Instead, I got a whole new life and I would have paid a thousand times the amount for it.

## 91.

# Your relationship with your opponent teaches you about yourself

Fighters encounter the same opponents over and over when they practice their techniques with their partners. They encounter different opponents if they compete in tournaments. (Sometimes these opponents are the same year after year, too, but you see them less often.) An opponent is different from an attacker, of course, and while an attacker can teach you about yourself, it is sincerely hoped that you'll never have to have the opportunity for this self-understanding.

But by competing with partners and opponents, you can learn about yourself. In the ring, there is no consensus building. There are two fighters, each of whom wants to win. This is not the stupid win-at-all-costs mentality where you decimate the landscape and then proudly survey the burnt-out wreckage you've acquired. No, this should be a simple passion for and enjoyment of winning. You can acquire this passion, and the assertive, maybe even aggressive, instinct that goes with it. But if you don't have it and you don't want it, that tells you something about yourself. (No, I'm not going to tell you that it means you're a loser! It probably means you're a consensus builder.)

If you do have that stupid win-at-all-costs mentality, you have some work to do. If you have to cheat to win, then you haven't actually won no matter what the scoreboard says. And you know that, so your self-image has to suffer, although you may not realize it at first. Win-at-all-costs is damaging psychologically and socially. It emphasizes the wrong values and it closes off opportunities to learn.

If you lose, and you blame the referee, or you blame your opponent for using unfair or illegal tactics, that tells you something about yourself. It means you don't want to admit that you lost, that you could lose. Losing is regarded in such negative terms that we don't want to think ourselves capable of it. But the person who is better than everyone else all the time doesn't exist. All of us have more skills and talent than some people sometimes and less than other people other times. So we're going to lose, now and then. Fact. Big deal.

If you lose, and the blame rightfully belongs on the referee—you should, in fact, have won—then instead of grousing about the unfairness of the verdict, set your sights on becoming so good that you defeat your opponents so obviously that no one would dare say otherwise. Will you ever really get this good? Maybe not. But it puts the focus on how you could become better, which is under your control, rather than on using a lot of negative energy to fume at the referees. (Olympic pairs figure-skating gold medals notwithstanding, you're not going to change the outcome of any athletic competition by complaining.)

If you lose, and sulk, and refuse to shake the opponent's hand, that tells you something. It tells you that you need to grow up. If you lose and obsess about the loss for the next three years, that should tell you something. It should tell you to get a life. If you lose and feel sad or upset about it, but can shake your opponent's hand and hit the gym with renewed determination the next day, that's telling you that you're a grown-up with the right attitude.

If you can laugh and joke with your opponent outside the ring, it means you have the right perspective. You should be able to get in the ring and do your best to win without having to personally "hate" your opponent or get mad at him. Your relationship with your opponent teaches you about yourself.

## Exercise

It's common in politics and other venues to publicly denigrate your opponent and then go to dinner with him. That's just politics. I don't endorse this type of behavior—I think we should be courteous and respectful to our opponents at all times—but it illustrates the point that you can want to defeat someone or argue about his views without having to hate him.

Try to keep your relations with opponents civil. This does not mean you should trust them or that you shouldn't want to win. It just means that you should be civil. You can't take it personally just because someone else wants the CEO position. They want to defeat you, yes, but not for the purpose of defeating you. They want to defeat you for the purpose of becoming CEO. So even if the opponent is not civil to you, you can see that it's not about you personally. If you're a good sport, people will see and appreciate that about you. No one appreciates a bad sport.

## 92

# Protect and nurture the beginner

A boxer once described her first sparring experience during training as a "brutal assault." A trainer, coach or instructor who would allow this to happen is guilty of assault himself or herself. Throwing a beginner into the ring, sink or swim, is a perversion of the teaching process. The beginner must always be protected and nurtured.

In a responsible *dojo,* the beginner is taught the techniques and is shown how to apply them in a closely supervised setting. Only after the beginner has developed skills and confidence does she begin to spar with partners, again under close supervision, with no contact. As skills and confidence increase, the amount of contact, speed and power used will increase. Each fighter always has the option of asking the other fighter to use more control. A fighter always has the option of bowing out of the match. The instructor still supervises, even at the black-belt level, to ensure that if two fighters are unevenly matched, no one gets hurt and that the inferior fighter is not overwhelmed by the superior fighter's skill.

As the beginner learns the techniques and forms, he is encouraged by the instructor and other students. While mistakes will be corrected, the emphasis is on the positive—what the student is doing right. Over time, his techniques will improve.

The instructor controls the amount of information directed at the beginner so he doesn't feel overwhelmed.

Stages of learning are divided into distinct levels. Most martial arts have a belt-ranking system to show when each student has learned the techniques for each level— "learned," not "mastered" them; mastery takes years.

The beginner learns at his own pace. Some beginners have trouble memorizing forms. There's no penalty for this. No one gets booted out of class because they're too slow learning. The journey is a journey, not a race. By protecting and nurturing the beginner, the instructor (and the school and other students) ensure that he will become a good martial artist. Protecting and nurturing the beginner helps martial artists stay with the program, even though the program is challenging, because all that nurturing and protecting helps develop trust among the members of this specific martial arts community.

In our lives, we are often beginners, and we should be protected and nurtured. Sometimes we have to demand this. When possible, we should take advantage of opportunities to be protected and nurtured, instead of dismissing them and thinking we'll be fine on our own. For instance, colleges usually have a new-student orientation session in the summer before fall classes start. Many students never take advantage of these sessions, then feel bewildered, uncertain and frustrated when they arrive on campus and try to find their dorm room.

We're also responsible for protecting and nurturing the beginners in our presence. A new trainee at work can have a positive experience when you show her around, or you can give her a negative experience by badmouthing all the co-workers and bosses.

Identify the beginners in your life. They might be your children. They might be other people's children. They might be a new in-law who needs to feel welcomed to the family. Or a new employee at work you could take to lunch even if it's not your job. Even if she's not in your department. Make it your responsibility to protect and nurture the beginner, then take delight in watching her blossom and grow, knowing you had a hand in it.

## 93

# Being a warrior is not about fighting, it is about finding the Truth

Sometimes it seems as if a warrior exists only to fight. But being a warrior is about finding the Truth, and you don't have to throw a punch to do that. A warrior is a person who finds the Way and follows the Way; who exhibits courage in the face of danger and fear, whether that courage is emotional or physical. A warrior can be a man or a woman, young or old, sprouting muscles or boasting none at all.

Being a warrior is a way of living. It's about being strong and determined in the pursuit of Truth. It is about living with integrity even when you're tempted to lie or cheat. (Why not? Everyone else is doing it . . . everyone but the warriors.)

A warrior faces each day with resolve, and optimism, even if the warrior knows it's going to be a dreadful day.

Warriors don't moan and bitch and whine and complain about the way things are or the way they should be. They do what they can to make things better. They know life isn't perfect, but that it's full of joy anyway. They are guided in their lives by their search for Truth, which they seek by following the Way.

Warriors incorporate the Way into their daily lives by keeping themselves open to growing, by being willing to undergo enlightening experiences and by taking risks.

### Exercise

Forget the idea that you have to punch people to be a warrior. Vow to live your life with warrior spirit—with commitment, determination and passion. Don't be satisfied by a mediocre, colorless existence. Know that you are a warrior, and start living the Way. Realize that you're trying to find the Truth, and less important matters are put in their proper perspective.

## 94
# The master does what is right without speaking

When the martial artist must act, she does so. Because she lives rightly, with integrity, her actions require little thought. She just does them. If she needs to intervene in a fight, she does. If she needs to expose a crime, she does.

She does not need to talk about what she's doing. She doesn't need to explain herself or get someone else's approval first. She knows she's responsible for right action. She also knows that she's a role model. She has students and friends and colleagues and family members who look up to her. She must model the correct behavior for them.

She does what is right without drawing attention to herself. She does not say, "Look at me! See how generous and kind I am!" She does not call the local television news station to come and cover her right action.

She does what is right even if there is a personal cost. She does what is right even if she doesn't like the people involved. She does what is right even if other people don't support her. She does what is right even when others try to undermine her and it would be easier not to act at all.

### Exercise

You are a master. You know what is right. Now go do it.

## 95
## Strive to be impervious to darkness and to fear

A warrior is not immune to fear. She feels fear. She just does not allow it to touch her or affect what she does. She may have moments of darkness—pessimism, unhappiness, doubt—but she does not allow these to rule her life. She affirms life instead of falling into despair.

This is easier said than done. There are times when life swings a baseball bat upside your head. There are times when your hands are shaking so badly from fear that you can't hold a glass of water . . . and I'm telling you to be impervious to those feelings.

Yes. Acknowledge them, accept that they're there and move along. One of the ways to grow stronger is to face your fears frequently. Then you learn that you can perform despite your fears. Your fears become more manageable when this happens.

Confront your fear and plan for it. If you know you'll be nervous asking your boss for a raise, and you're afraid you'll blow it when he looks at you sternly and demands, "What have you done to deserve a raise?" then you can prepare for that. Rehearse what you will say and the various responses he might make. It isn't going too far to enlist a friend to play your boss and critique your performance.

You can practice calming techniques. Deep breathing, meditation and visualization can all help you overcome your fear so that you can perform.

When you're facing darkness rather than fear, the unhappy clammy feeling you have in your heart can be harder to deal with than fear. You know what you're afraid of, so you can calm yourself down, and you can practice how you're going to react to fear.

But in the realms of darkness, you can't simply face your fear and do it anyway, because there's no "it" to do. There's just a feeling of unhappiness or doubt or ennui. To be impervious to darkness requires a slightly different strategy. Sometimes what starts our feelings of self-doubt spiralling out of control is an event—a criticism or an insult. A party you gave and no one came. It's easy to start feeling sorry for yourself. In fact, you're perfectly justified in feeling sorry for yourself and no one would fault you for it (except me).

The fact is, we all give parties to which no one comes. This means that it is *not* a national tragedy when it happens to you. Instead, keep a sense of perspective. See if you can find something to laugh at. If someone's cutting comment hurt your feelings, hold a contest among your friends for the worst insult ever received. Go look at yourself in the mirror when you're feeling down. Nothing like seeing that pouting lip thrust out to make you laugh.

Distract yourself. You distract a crying baby by giving him a toy; you can distract yourself from obsessing over the darkness by going for a walk, reading a good book, going to a movie with a friend, cleaning your kid's bedroom, lifting weights.

Repeat affirmations. If someone said you're a fat slob, don't let that comment get written into your brain, which is what will happen if you keep repeating to yourself and others, "I can't believe she called me a fat slob! Can you believe she called me a fat slob?" Pretty soon your brain is thinking, "I'm a fat slob." Tell yourself repeatedly, "I'm a skinny slob," or "I'm a relaxed, happy person," even if the truth is you are slightly overweight. Affirmations work even when they're not true, that's the magic of them. If someone calls you a fat slob, and you tell yourself, "I'm a slender, active person," that's what you'll believe. And you may actually start acting like one. You can rephrase the attack. "Karen must be terribly insecure to insult me like that. I feel sorry for her."

Sometimes you can't nail down the reason for your

darkness like this. There's no specific injury or problem that you have, you're just sunk into a funk. Obviously, if you're depressed you need to see a doctor. Medication and counseling may help. But if you're feeling just a general malaise about the world, it's best not to give in to it. (That's often how real depression starts. It can be a gradual slide from the blues to clinical depression. It's possible to stop the blues from becoming something more dire if you take the problem seriously and take action immediately.)

Give yourself alternatives. Accept that you're not the most joyful person in the world today, but don't let that stop you from doing your daily job and handling your life as normally as possible. Don't beat yourself up because today was not your sunniest day ever.

### Exercise

It requires discipline to live your life impervious to darkness and fear. Understand that you have many gifts and life is worth living. Give. Although that seems counterintuitive—we tend to want to *take* when we're down—the act of giving makes us feel good and worthy and needed. Volunteer at the local humane society or at a nursing home or hospital. You will be reminded of all you have to feel grateful for and you'll see that you're necessary.

## 96

# Do not look back once the Path is chosen

When I began training in the martial arts, I knew I had found the Way. Martial arts saved my life. I knew that. I was grateful for it. My training meant everything to me. I worked out repeatedly throughout the week. Because of my commitment, I kicked my nicotine addiction for good. I started eating better and lost weight. My academic work also improved—I was more disciplined and committed to my studies. I even got along better with my family, although they thought my hobby was an odd one.

I knew I was on the right Path. But, as a beginner, I kept looking back to my old life with longing. As I was headed out the door to go train in the evening, I had visions of curling up on the sofa with a good book, eating a huge batch of buttered popcorn.

Now, it wasn't that I couldn't do that every now and then—nothing about the Way says you can't eat popcorn—it was just that I had this longing *all the time.* Every single day. I didn't really want to be sitting on the sofa, but all the changes I had made were scary, and the thought was comforting.

But it was interfering with my progress.

Finally, I said goodbye to my comfortable old life and stopped worrying about the changes. After all, if the changes proved too horrendous, I could always change back.

Do not look backward once the Path is chosen. Commit yourself to the Path and welcome the changes. The twinges of discomfort you feel will go away, unless, of course, it's a pulled hamstring you're feeling, and then you'll have to rest.

During all our life changes, it's best to look forward and not back. The change has been made; ensure that it's a good change. If you're getting married, don't spend all your time reminiscing about how much fun it was to be single. If you want to be single, stay single. If you want to be married, think married. Think of all the wonderful things you'll do now that you're married that you couldn't do or wouldn't do when you were single. When you have a child, don't dwell on the fact that you were able to sleep eight hours straight before children. Concentrate on the present, focus on the here and now. Make a plan or two about the future, but stop looking back.

### Exercise

One of the reasons we look back is because the future is uncertain. We don't know what will happen and it might be something horrible. The past, on the other hand, is not scary. We know how it turned out. We're familiar with it. Even if bad things happened in it, those bad things are over now.

Live in the moment. Once you have chosen the Way, you have chosen the present. Focus on what you're doing now. An occasional peek into the future is acceptable but not mandatory, especially if the future looks scary. Take care of today, and tomorrow will take care of itself. Take care of today, and don't dwell on yesterday.

## 97

# The warrior must be single-minded

The warrior knows that to defeat the attacker, he cannot be distracted by the bruise he just got on his shin or what's for dinner tonight. He focuses on a single thought: Defeat the attacker.

In the ring, the fighter knows that to defeat the opponent, she cannot be distracted by the yelling of the spectators, the fact that the last time she fought this opponent she lost, or the vibrant blue eyes of the center-ring judge. She focuses on a single thought: Win the match.

The warrior must be single-minded.

More important, the warrior must be single-minded about the right thing. It's no use the warrior being single-minded about how much the last punch hurt . . . it won't get him what he wants, which is to defeat the attacker.

In our lives, we often have multiple goals and desires, and we want to fulfill them all at the same time. We want to be a good parent, a good spouse and a good child; and we want to succeed in our career, earn an advanced degree in night school and start our own business; and we want to lose weight and get into shape; and we want to live frugally and develop frugal habits so we can save up to buy a house.

No wonder we're tired at the end of the day, and yet still feel frustrated and unfulfilled, as if we were *never* going to reach our goals.

Now, certainly it is possible to have more than one goal, but they must be compatible goals. And they must not all require the same amount of energy at the same time. Succeeding in your career and starting a business are probably not compatible goals. At some point they will conflict, unless the business you're starting is just something simple like selling stuff from Grandma's attic on e-Bay. But if you're going to both succeed in your computer programming career and start your own software company (of which you will be president and CEO), and you want that company to rival Microsoft, which is where you happen to be employed, at some point conflict between the two goals will inevitably arise.

This does not mean you can't be employed and start your own business on the side. It just means you'll focus on your business and not your job (other than fulfilling your obligations such as showing up and doing your work).

Every January, many of us start on self-improvement plans that are destined to fail because we're trying to do too much at once. We vow to be better parents, better lovers, better employees, and we vow to lose weight, learn Sanskrit and build a house by hand. Six weeks later, all of our plans have been abandoned and no goal has been reached.

Start with one or two compatible goals. Build from there. Some goals will be ongoing (I will always try to be a good mother to my daughter) and some will reach a conclusion. (Once I earned my Ph.D., it was mine to keep and required no additional effort.)

Choose what you need to do right now, then be single-minded about accomplishing your objective.

What are your life goals? What do you need to accomplish them, to feel satisfied? When you're dying, what is the one thing you'll regret not doing? Or the one thing you'll say with satisfaction, "I'm glad I did that"? Make a list of these life goals. Choose one or two, and dedicate yourself, single-mindedly, to achieving them. The others will get their turn.

If you have ten life goals, rank them in order of importance. Do the most important ones first. Taking steps toward too many goals at once will distract you from reaching any of your goals.

## 98
# You are the *kata*, and the *kata* is beautiful

Traditional martial artists learn forms (the Japanese word is *kata*), which are patterns of techniques that you memorize. *Kata* exists for several purposes—to help you perfect your technique, to show you how to put different techniques together, to help you practice moving from one technique to another (and from one direction to another). The *kata* also helps you improve your agility and balance. Forms also teach you how to rely on body memory. Once you memorize a form, you can't think too much about what comes next, or you will interrupt the flow. You'll be turning a physical exercise into an intellectual one. If you just trust your body to remember what happens next, it will. Usually.

This is important because you're training your body to have an automatic physical response. In the ring, you don't want to have to think about every move you're going to make. "Okay, gotta block that punch. Oh, look, incoming . . . now there's an opening, maybe I should kick." Instead, you want the techniques to flow without a lot of intellectualizing. The practice of forms helps you accomplish this.

If someone grabs you on the street, you want to be able to respond automatically. You don't want to think, "Oh, my stars and whiskers! I'm being attacked! Now what? Maybe I should try an elbow strike to the solar plexus? No, wait, a back kick to the knee might be more effective given my position." *Kata* helps your techniques become more automatic. You learn how to use more than one technique in a row, which is also helpful both in the ring and on the street.

All of that is very nice, but you could probably learn as much by just practicing the techniques repeatedly with a partner. So why the *kata*?

The *kata* shows off your grace and power and agility. It requires your best effort and your most intense concentration.

The *kata* is beautiful. But the *kata* is also a dance, and just as you cannot separate the dancer from the dance, you cannot separate the *kata* from the person who performs it. You are the *kata*. If the *kata* is beautiful, so are you.

The *kata* is like a beautiful song. It has its own special language. It's like a dance, but it uses warrior movements. It's like sparring, but it's done solo. The fighter is turned inward, focusing only on trying to express himself or herself as perfectly as possible.

In all creative pursuits, there is an opportunity for oneness with the creation. The musician making music, the writer spinning stories, the painter creating images. All of these acts are beautiful—the acts and the actors. All of them allow the performer, the doer, to connect with something larger, more universal, something outside themselves. In the moment of performance, transformation occurs. You are the *kata*, and the *kata* is beautiful.

### Exercise

An unwritten poem can never move a reader's spirit. Be certain to write your poems. Nurture your creativity. This can take many outlets—writing, dancing and painting are only the obvious ones. Some people create with food or fabric. Allow yourself the opportunity and space to feel at one with your creative work. Don't be embarrassed to say "that's beautiful" about your own creative work. Know that this reflects well on you.

### 99
## Consult your intuition before taking action

Much of what a warrior learns is control. She learns to control her fear so that she can perform. She learns to manage her anger and doubt so that she can make the right decision. Much of what a warrior must do is based on a logical, rational process. You decide on a goal. You devise a strategy and tactics. You meet the goal. You move on to the next thing.

A warrior also trains to react without thinking at all. There's no "Here comes a punch; better block it." The punch comes, it is blocked.

But a warrior also knows that she must consult her intuition before taking action. (Once the punch is blocked, that is.)

We don't trust our intuition partly because modern society debunks it, partly because we don't understand it and partly because we don't train it.

Humans are animals. Animals have instincts. But society overlays certain behaviors on these instincts. For example, we discourage humans from mating in the streets. (This, no doubt, is a good thing.)

Your intuition is made up of such animal instincts, and if you can peel away some of that civilization for a moment, you can listen to your instincts. Your body knows when someone is watching you. You know when you're home alone. The house feels empty. You also know when you're not alone.

Along with instincts, your intuition is made up of past references, knowledge and impressions about the world that you may not even know you have formed. Your intuition tells you about the world—your perspective of the world. So it's always best to consult your intuition before taking action.

We know that there are rational ways to make decisions. This house or that one? We can make a list of pros and cons for each house and choose logically. (This even works sometimes.) But no amount of rational decision-making will make us happy about moving into a house we have an irrational dislike for. Our instincts will usually tell us that this particular feature of a house is likely to drive us nuts, or that kitchen feels just right for entertaining guests.

Maybe you don't have guests, your rational mind tells you. But if you choose the house with that kitchen, maybe you would. Maybe your intuition is telling you it's time for more friendly gatherings.

When your intuition tells you to turn down a job, listen to it long and hard before accepting the job. And don't be too surprised if you're out looking for another job soon. When your heart whispers "This is the one!" throw caution to the wind and choose the oatmeal bread over the whole wheat.

## Exercise

To cultivate your intuition, simply start consulting it. If you feel uneasy about a situation, ask yourself what factors are contributing. Suppose a friend sets up a blind date. You agree, then begin to feel uneasy. Maybe you're just afraid you'll have a terrible time. Maybe you're afraid that this will be the right man for you and you just don't want to get into that kind of relationship right now. Maybe you're afraid he doesn't know what "no" means. You have a couple of options, so plan accordingly. You can cancel the date. If you're afraid of wasting your time, meet for lunch instead of dinner or a cup of coffee instead of a movie. Don't allow your friend to give out personal information about you. Don't do it yourself until you've met the guy and have had at least one long conversation. Prepare an escape plan. Go to the restroom, call a friend and have her call you in ten minutes on your cell phone, inventing an emergency. Be willing to have a blinding headache, if needed.

If your intuition is telling you a certain job is not right for you, ask if you could job shadow for a day or two to make certain your skills and their expectations are compatible. Ask friends what they know about the company. Don't give too much weight to disgruntled former employees, but keep their comments in mind.

Finally, even if it's totally irrational to fall in love with a floppy-eared six-week-old malamute puppy you had no intention of adopting, go ahead and do it anyway.

## 100
## Triumph

Live like a warrior and you will triumph in the end.

# Conclusion

When I first stepped into the *dojo* more than ten years ago, I did not know that I was going to learn to live like a warrior. I didn't know that it would change my life. I didn't even plan to start martial arts. I planned to run errands.

As it so happened, I was in graduate school, overweight and out of shape. I had recently been hospitalized with a collapsed lung, and the doctor had said to me, "If you don't quit smoking, you're going to die." Since I was only twenty-six years old, and I wanted to live past thirty, I took his advice and quit smoking, which was a lot harder than it sounds.

A few months after I quit, I found myself getting fatter and grumpier by the day. I could feel my determination falter; I knew I was going to start smoking again if I didn't do something drastic. So I went on a diet. This lasted just shy of two hours. Then I decided what I really needed to do was get some exercise, so I thought about walking, but going for a walk in the middle of a Kansas summer day is for mad dogs and Englishmen. Alternatively, I realized, I could sign up for an aerobics class. But the idea of bouncing around in a spandex leotard made me want a cigarette even more.

Then I got the bright idea that I could bring a bottle of wine to my friend Susan's house, and sharing it with her would make me feel better.

So I drove over to the strip mall where the liquor store

was located, and as I was walking down the sidewalk, I noticed the sign: New Horizons Black Belt Academy of Tae Kwon Do. I stopped dead in my tracks. I had known the place was there; it wasn't far from where I lived. But I had just never thought of it in relationship to me before. On impulse, I walked in. There was a tiny blonde woman sitting behind the desk, wearing a white uniform with a black belt. I said, brilliantly, "So, uh, you teach Tae Kwon Do here?" I wasn't even sure what Tae Kwon Do was, but I had the sense that it involved Karate chops and kicking people in the shin, which seemed like a hell of a lot more fun than doing step aerobics to Madonna songs.

"Yes," she said.

And I said, "I want to sign up," which I hadn't known I wanted until the words came out of my mouth.

So I left the school, clutching my brand-new uniform and a class schedule, and I completely forgot about the liquor store. I started training that very day, and a few weeks later, I tested for my yellow belt. I was extremely nervous. I had to show that I knew ten basic techniques, and that I could perform two forms, and that I knew the definition of Tae Kwon Do and how to count to ten in Korean.

At the test, the judge asked a fellow student, "Have you ever had to use your Tae Kwon Do training?" And the student said, "No, sir, I haven't."

The judge said, "You should use your Tae Kwon Do training every day of your life."

At first, I did not realize what he meant. I thought maybe he was referring to the self-defense training that teaches us to walk away from violent confrontation when we can. I thought maybe he was talking about coming to class every day.

It took some time before I realized he simply meant you should use your training every day of your life. That's the Way of martial arts.

The Way in your life may not take you to a martial arts school en route to the liquor store, but if you're open to it, you will go places you never dreamed you'd see. And you'll live like the warrior you always knew you were.

# FOR THE BEST IN PAPERBACKS, LOOK FOR THE 🐧

In every corner of the world, on every subject under the sun, Penguin represents quality and variety—the very best in publishing today.

For complete information about books available from Penguin—including Penguin Classics, Penguin Compass, and Puffins—and how to order them, write to us at the appropriate address below. Please note that for copyright reasons the selection of books varies from country to country.